DISCERNING THE SIGNS OF THE TIMES

T0339162

DISCERNING THE SIGNS OF THE TIMES

The Vision of Elisabeth Behr-Sigel

~

Edited by

MICHAEL PLEKON & SARAH E. HINLICKY

*Translations by Lyn Breck, Michael Plekon,
Deno Takles, and Rachel Mortimer*

ST VLADIMIR'S SEMINARY PRESS
CRESTWOOD, NEW YORK
2001

Library of Congress Cataloging-in-Publication Data
Behr-Sigel, Elisabeth.
  Discerning the signs of the times : the vision of Elisabeth Behr-Sigel / edited by
Michael Plekon and Sarah E. Hinlicky ; translations by Lyn Breck ... [et al.].
    p. cm.
  ISBN 0-88141-218-X (alk. paper)
    1. Women in the Orthodox Eastern Church.   2. Ordination of women—
Orthodox Eastern Church.   3. Orthodox Eastern Church—Doctrines.   4. Or-
thodox Eastern Church—Membership.   I. Plekon, Michael, 1948- II. Hinlicky,
Sarah E.   III. Title.
BX342.5 .B43 2001
281.9 09 04—dc21

                                                                    00-67365

Copyright © 2001
ST VLADIMIR'S SEMINARY PRESS
575 Scarsdale Rd., Crestwood, NY 10707
1-800-204-2665

ISBN 0-88141-218-X

PRINTED IN THE UNITED STATES OF AMERICA

Acknowledgements

First and foremost, we thank Dr Elisabeth Behr-Sigel herself for permission to assemble this collection, for her suggestions about its contents, and for sharing her life and thinking with us. Thanks then must go to Lyn Breck who not only translated several essays but also contributed the biographical essay and who was, together with Phil Tamoush, really the heart and soul, the prime mover of the entire project. Sarah E. Hinlicky both contributed an essay and did the final editing and proof-reading of the text. Hannah Plekon assisted in text transmission.

For the composition of the biography of Dr Behr-Sigel, special thanks go to her daughter Nadine Arnoud and her son-in-law, Fr Jean Marie Arnoud. Fr Boris Bobrinskoy, Dean of St Sergius Theological Institute in Paris and Matushka Hélène were also valuable contributors. Professor Sophie Deicha, also of St Sergius Institute provided information regarding Dr Behr-Sigel's current influence on the role of women in the Church.

Since it has been published in bishop Kallistos Ware and Elisabeth Behr-Sigel, *The Ordination of Women in the Orthodox Church* (Geneva: WCC, 2000), Elizabeth Behr-Sigel's most recent article, "The Ordination of Women, a Question Also Posed to the Orthodox Churches," does not appear here.

Elisabeth Behr-Sigel's vision of the Church is one of a communion, a community of men and women, clergy and laity, joined in the joy and peace of the Holy Trinity, God One-in-three, the very icon of unity and community. The work on this collection has truly been a labor of love for a singular "Mother of the Church" in our time as well as an experience of community for all of us who were engaged in it. We were privileged to have been able to do it and are grateful for the life and witness of Elisabeth Behr-Sigel, who entered her 94th year of life on 21 July 2000, the feast-day, in the Eastern Church, of the great prophet Ezekiel and the eve of the feast of that holy myrrhbearer and "Equal to the Apostles," one of the first witnesses to Christ's resurrection, St Mary Magdalene. How fitting that this was the day of Elisabeth's birth. "Many years."

Contents

Preface

by Fr Michel Evdokimov[*]

The essays in this collection, which I have the great joy of presenting to English-speaking readers, were written by an elderly, and in size very small, but great lady, endowed with a lively intelligence and a memory as solid as rock. She really is our "living memory" of Orthodoxy in the twentieth century. She possesses an uncommon vitality, a capacity for openness, and a compassion toward her neighbor, all of which have made her one of the most attractive personalities in the Orthodox Church in France, and beyond that in Europe, in these last decades. Above all, if you had had the honor, as I did, of being held in her arms on the day of your baptism—but enough of that, for she promised me that she would not begin that way again.

She is a great witness of the encounter between France (and the West more generally) and Russia. Born in Strasbourg in 1907, she seemed destined from the start of her studies at the Protestant faculty of theology to enter the pastoral ministry, for which she already had received a commission to serve temporarily in a parish. Instead, she eventually became a professor of philosophy. After her retirement from this post, and from the momentum of an international gathering of Orthodox women (the first of its kind ever) at the Agapia Monastery in Romania, in 1976, she suddenly felt herself ready to launch out into an expansive reflection on the place of women in the Church. She attempted, with tact and firmness, to address the audacious challenge of modernity leveled at the Orthodox and Catholic Churches concerning the possible access of women to the ministerial priesthood. Whatever one's personal opinion on this question, it is to Elisabeth Behr-Sigel's credit that she has brought this challenge into the consciousness of the Orthodox. She is

* Son of Theologian Paul Evdokimov, Fr Michel is professor emeritus of comparative literature at the University of Poitiers, an editor of the journals *Contacts* and *Service Orthodoxe de Presse*, secretary of the Orthodox Interepiscopal Committee in France, prolific author and rector of the parish of Châtenay-Malabry, outside Paris.

most prudent, not ignoring the weight of Tradition and the spontaneous negative reactions from ecclesiastical circles which are not always ready nor
equipped to respond to the challenge. However, she does invite one to rethink
and to reevaluate the role of women in the Church at all levels, and more particularly she has urged the Church once more to recognize the specific ministries of women, such as the order of deaconesses. She has herself exercised the
ministry of theological instruction at the St Sergius Institute in Paris. With
dedication she has served as a warden of her parish, which is also in Paris, and
for many years she has been a theological consultant to the assembly of
Orthodox bishops in France, today called the Interepiscopal Committee. Her
thinking about women has never remained merely theoretical, but flowed
from the reflection of a great lady who put her gifts and her self-sacrifice at the
service of the Church. Her actions have shown just how far, in the actual life
of the Orthodox Church, the words of St Paul about the royal priesthood of
all the faithful can really be put into practice, namely that every baptized
person has a priestly function to fulfill in the Church. "Not well known, the
face of woman in Orthodox Christianity still is there to be explored," she has
written with justification.

Behr-Sigel came to Orthodoxy through a series of events which played
significant roles in her life. First there was her marriage to a Russian, with
whom she had three children who themselves became deeply engaged in
the life of the Church. One of her daughters is the wife of a priest. Also
figuring importantly was her encounter with so many prestigious Russian
theologians, such as Fr Sergius Bulgakov, whom she keeps in radiant
remembrance, along with great spiritual teachers such as Fr Lev Gillet. She
has written an immense biography of him which retraces the life of this
monk of the Eastern Church as well as the life of the Orthodox Church
itself throughout the course of this century. One should not forget her
friendship of many years with the lay theologian Paul Evdokimov, with
whom she shared great enthusiasm for the idea of an "interiorized monasticism" (on this subject, see her essay, "A Monk in the City: Alexander
Bukharev," in this volume). Her own study of the history of the kenotic
dimension of Russian spirituality was a pioneering work of scholarship of
the Eastern Church in France (see "The Kenotic, the Humble Christ").
Compelled by the need to undertand modernity, conscious of the limited
witness that an impoverished, oppressed Orthodox Church could offer, a
Church often turned in upon itself, she has always desired to think about
the world in the light in which she sees it, that is, in the light of Christ

and the Gospel. Among the many facets of her rich personality, one can rightly underscore the importance of the Bible, the evangelical dimension of the Christian faith. Such a perspective is constantly necessary in a Church often carried away by ritualism. It is vital to remind this Church that the liturgical rites are themselves deeply rooted in the very bedrock of the Scriptures (see "The Bible, Tradition, the Sacraments"). In this return to the evangelical sources of life she is very close to Fr Lev Gillet, who carried in himself the love and compassion of Christ after having had a singular experience, a dazzling ecstasy as it were, on the shore of Lake Tiberias in the Holy Land. Impassioned about the great questions which have arisen in our age, Behr-Sigel herself was compelled to be completely open to the efforts of other churches to respond to these issues in common within ecumenical relationships. Thus, she has been untiring in leading conferences, giving papers and talks at innumerable gatherings of Christians of various ecclesial traditions, and in giving courses at ISEO, the Graduate Institute of Ecumenical Studies. She also became the Orthodox vice-president of "ACAT," Christian Action for the Abolition of Torture.

These few remarks are meant to introduce you, if only modestly yet also intimately to a great lady of warmth and light, truly our leading elder, who herself witnesses to the irreplaceable ministry that women are able to exercise and, I will say, should exercise in the Church. The articles and other selections from various books assembled here lead into the vast horizon of her thinking which is at one and the same time open to the great questions of modernity while never ceasing to be solidly based on Tradition. It is to Elisabeth Behr-Sigel that we should go to trace the broad outlines of the task which awaits Orthodox theology at the dawn of the third millennium, and for exactly that reason she was invited to speak at the inauguration of the Institute of Orthodox Theology at Cambridge (see "Orthodox Theological Formation in the 21st Century: The Tasks involved"). Last but not least, all of these writings bear the mark of finesse, of a style which has savor, of a richness and elegance rare among those who push the theological pen, the style of which Buffon would say, "it is the man himself," or rather, "the woman herself."

We affectionately call Elisabeth Behr-Sigel our "mother" in the Church. Probably this is because, despite her more than ninety years of age, she has managed to remain forever young in her person and in her thought, and this she will continue to be.

Introduction

by Sarah E. Hinlicky

Elisabeth Behr-Sigel is a theologian who thinks in universal terms. Her universal thinking is both rare and brave in a day when universal truth claims are scorned and theology tends toward the idiosyncratic. Furthermore, her universality is rare and brave for one so deeply involved in the ecumenical movement. It often seems that ecumenism, for all its good intentions in theory, degenerates in reality into lowest common denominator Christianity, unity in spite of Christ rather than because of him. Behr-Sigel's universality is one without such this-worldly compromises. Her ecumenicity stems from her confidence that all the various splintered churches, in being what they truly are, can both learn from and inform one another of the full truth in Christ Jesus. None of this entails compromise, for compromise somehow indicates a lack of integrity. But throughout the difficulty and disagreeableness of debate, Behr-Sigel stands out as one who believes wholeheartedly that the Spirit will lead the broken body of the Church into wholeness again.

In particular, it is Behr-Sigel's self-named "*apatheia*" toward ecumenism—apathy in the sense of abandoning tenacious clinging to one's own efforts—that makes her so infinitely valuable to the ecumenical debate over the ordination of women. At a juncture in Christian history when claims about women from either side of the argument provoke strong reactions, Behr-Sigel remains determinedly moderate, even-handed, unpolemical, and wisely reserved. She has done her work for the Church; now she leaves it to the Church to decide. And yet for all her mildness about this very provocative issue, Behr-Sigel does burn with zeal—for the Gospel. For all her tolerance of the many voices participating in the discussion, she is finally intolerant of anything that obscures the purity of the word of salvation through God's only Son. This pairing of apathy and zeal (devotion to God from a to z!) permits her to sift through the wheats and tares on each side of the debate, both to criticize and congratulate either perspective. And in all the modesty of her ninety-some years, she is willing to do the same with her own conclusions.

In spite of all her ecumenical encounters, especially with the World Council of Churches, Behr-Sigel writes mainly for an Orthodox audience. As such, her task is to provide the initial encounter with arguments in favor of ordained women to a church that does not allow women in any of the threefold offices (though there are signs that the female diaconate may be reinstated). However, her work is of value not only to the Orthodox who are confronting this issue for the first time. Despite the practice of ordaining women in the Reformation churches for several decades or more now, the issue is still a live one. Behr-Sigel's writings, saturated in the Tradition of the East, wrestle afresh with a concern very close to the heart of Protestants. At the same time, they provide for Western readers a lively and new—or perhaps very old—perspective, one closely aligned with the patristic writers and thinkers. It makes for a happy marriage; the Protestant churches have always sought to be faithful to the early roots of the Christian Church. Put into contemporary terms and addressing very modern issues, Behr-Sigel calls to Protestant minds again such theological matters as the sacramental character of the ordained offices and the calling of the priest to be a living icon of Christ. It would be a fair exchange indeed if the Reformation churches were to consider seriously again these ancient teachings about the ordained ministry, for Behr-Sigel (along with her good friend, Paul Evdokimov) has done much to enrich Orthodox theology of the laity in her commitment to the priesthood of all believers, a more typically Protestant emphasis.

Elisabeth Behr-Sigel's works are something like a bottomless treasure chest. She is usually discovered by those interested in the churchly ministry of women within Orthodoxy. And yet once she has given generously of her intellectual efforts in that area, she leads her readers further and deeper into the broader problem at stake, the problem of modernity. Behr-Sigel's desire to explore the role of women in the Church is the best known manifestation of her deeper concern, tied again to her search for universality, which is the problem of modernity. With the courage of faith and intellectual honesty working together, she has faced modernity and has called on other Eastern Christians to do the same, to overcome all the noise and chaos and flashing lights that are too often assumed to be the primary and decidedly negative features of modernity. And she has not stopped at clearing away the distortions. Behr-Sigel has spent her life calling the Church to recognize the profound hope that it has been given in this new age: hope in the growing opportunities for solidarity among the nations, the reduction of ordinary everyday pain and high mortality rates from disease, ever-expanding educational resources, changing attitudes toward class and race, the hope for the reunion of the churches into the Church, the explosion of missionary outreach, and the development of countless Spirit-given charisms. These are the blessings of the modern world to which Behr-Sigel tirelessly calls the people of the Church to commit themselves, neither to cave in to the accompanying evils nor to reject the evils and blessings alike.

In other words, Elisabeth Behr-Sigel is an inspired reader of the signs of the times. The universal Church on earth would do well to listen to one of its contemporary universal teachers.

I

My Journey to the
Orthodox Church*

M y journey to the Orthodox Church began with my encounter with
the Russian emigration during the fervent climate of the beginnings
of the ecumenical movement. The Russian emigration was materially poor
but spiritually rich. It unfolded in Western Europe between the wars, starting
at the end of the Bolshevik revolution of 1917.

It is well known that I am originally Protestant. As an infant, I was
baptized in the Lutheran Church of Alsace-Lorraine to which my father
belonged by family tradition.[1] My mother was Jewish, from an assimilated
and liberal, almost to the point of agnostic, family from the former
Austro-Hungarian Empire. From this same background comes the
founder of psychoanalysis, Sigmund Freud, with whom my maternal
grandmother not only shared a native village but also the same last name.
Without being totally non-believers, my parents were detached from all
religious practice. In spite of or maybe because of that, I was a worried
adolescent, tormented by eternal metaphysical problems.

Around the age of sixteen, I joined a Protestant youth group which was
open to all young Christians. We had adopted for a motto the prayer of
Christ for his disciples in John 17:21, "that they may all be one." It is in this
environment, to which I owe immense gratitude, that I heard addressed to
me personally the call of Jesus: "You, follow me." Despite my infidelities
to it, that call has never ceased to ring in me.

Because theological studies were not yet open to women, I began with
philosophy. But in 1926 the University of Strasbourg accepted its first female
students of theology. I was one of these the following year. Ironically, it is in
this Protestant framework that I made my first contact with the Orthodox
Church. Among my fellow students were some Orthodox on scholarship and

* To be published in a forthcoming issue of the *St Nina Quarterly*. Translated by Deno Takles.

among them two Russian émigrés. One of them was, like myself, passionate about the ecumenical dialogue which was just then beginning. He introduced me to the *sobornost* of the great nineteenth-century Russian theologian, Alexis Khomiakov—a vision of Church unity as communion, the free accord of the consciences in faith and love, an accord in some ways musical. The Slavic word *sobornost* etymologically signifies "conciliation," but it is sometimes translated by the neologism, "symphonicity."[2]

In opposition to the concept of judicial and authoritarian unity of the Roman Catholic Church as well as the Protestant libertarian individualism, *sobornost* enchanted me and appeared to be a way out of these antinomies of western Christians. Even more profound was my impression at the Orthodox Paschal Vigil to which my new friends escorted me. Constantly repeated by the priest, the choir, and the faithful, the Paschal jubilation cry of "Christ is risen!" flooded my heart with joy. The light of the Resurrection dispersed all shadows, even the shadows I carried within. I decided that I had to make better acquaintance with this strange Orthodox Church, at the same time so old, so archaic, and so young and alive.

The opportunity presented itself the following year. During my studies at the Protestant faculty of theology in Paris, I was introduced, thanks to my friends, to the world of the Russian émigrés. For these émigrés, Paris had become the cultural and religious capital. With its great thinkers like the philosopher of creative liberty, Nikolai Berdiaev, Fr Sergius Bulgakov, a former Marxist who became a gifted Orthodox theologian and Dean of the St Sergius Institute of Orthodox Theology, their common friend Mother Maria Skobtsova, a prophetess of renewed monasticism, and some young theologians still unknown, Vladimir Lossky, Paul Evdokimov, and Evgraf Kovalevsky, who all became my friends, I discovered an Orthodoxy open to western thought, open to dialogue with the other churches yet still faithful to the essence of the Orthodox faith. In the catastrophe which had thrown them into an unknown land, these men and women found a divine call: to become intermediaries between the Christian East and West that had been tragically separated.

But the decisive encounter for me was with a Benedictine monk, Fr Lev Gillet, received into communion with the Orthodox Church several months earlier, a communion to which he aspired, pushed by a great love of holy Russia and a deep nostalgia for the undivided Church, for the one, holy, catholic, apostolic Church of the first centuries of which, it appeared to him, the Orthodox Church was heir.[3] I found in him a sure spiritual guide who helped me rid myself of internal conflicts. It is he who, without expecting me to deny the received graces of the Church into which I was baptized, united me by the sacrament of chrismation with the Orthodox Church.**

At the time of our meeting in 1929, Fr Lev Gillet, who often went by the name "A Monk of the Eastern Church," was in the process of starting up the first French-language Orthodox parish in France, with the blessing of Metropolitan Evlogii and the help of the young Russians mentioned above. The parish, dedicated to the Transfiguration and St Genevieve of Paris, was a small and fragile seed of the "western Orthodoxy" of which we dreamed. Such is the great hope of the light which we followed, my friends and I.

My pastoral ministry experience took place between 1931 and 1932. Already Orthodox on the inside, I had just passed the final exams for the theology department of the Protestant University of Strasbourg—even finished first in my class, what an honor for the young women! Invited by the Ecclesiastical Inspector (the equivalent of a bishop) of the Reformed Church, I was solicited by him to assume the ministry of "auxiliary pastor" in a modest parish in the country. Deprived of its pastor for some time, the parish of Ville-Climont suffered from this abandonment.

The experience constituted a risk, which the Inspector recognized. I was the first woman in France to be officially installed into such a ministry. But it was about reacting to a real and pressing need, and also to show that a woman was capable of rendering this service. I accepted. Was I wrong? I leave the judgment to the Lord, who, like the old Portuguese proverb quoted by Paul Claudel, "writes straight with our crooked lines." My acceptance should also be situated in the context of the times. Within the ecumenical dialogue which was barely beginning—a dialogue from which the Roman Catholic Church was still absent—the ordination of women had not yet become a major problem. Anyway, it was not a question of my "ordination." There would not be any "consecration." I would be delegated by the Reformed Church to offer a specific service. Courageously, the small Reformed Church of Alsace-Lorraine, the first in

** Translator's note: Madam Behr-Sigel was chrismated on December 13th, 1929. Her Bishop, Metropolitan Evlogii, gave his blessing for her to do the auxiliary pastorate at Ville-Climont, as delegated by the unusual emergency conditions in the post World War I years.

France—suffering like the rest of the churches from a shortage of pastors following the slaughter of the First World War—had attempted to reply to a serious question: what do women do who are educated in theology and aspire to the ministry? Its decision to integrate them into its pastoral corps appeared to me theologically well-founded, conforming to its theology of ministry. I admired its courage and I felt solidarity with my Protestant sisters. In the meantime, I did not ignore the fact that the problem was conceived in different terms within the framework of the sacramental and liturgical symbolism of the Orthodox Church. With terms of conciliatory reflection, according to the spirit of *sobornost*, would the Orthodox Church, one day, ordain women to the diaconate, even to the priesthood? I left the question open. For the moment, it was about a simple thing: to serve a Christian community which was calling me.

Nevertheless, it was not without apprehension that I, as the first woman in France to be called to the pastoral ministry, presented myself to my parishioners. Wouldn't they reject me? Wouldn't I be a "scandal" to them, like the guilty one in the letter of the apostle Paul (1 Cor 8:12-13)? It was nothing of the sort! I am still amazed today at the ease with which this parish accepted me. The parish recognized, I believe, that I was there to assure the regularity of Sunday worship from which they were deprived for so long, to proclaim the Gospel, to take charge of the religious instruction of the children and teenagers, and to visit the sick and the isolated, of which there were quite a few due to the fact that it was a mountainous region. The women, despite my youth, opened themselves up to me with their problems. But even the men respected me. I never felt attacked by a single word or hurtful attitude. Maybe, if the experience had been longer, I would have encountered difficulties. In fact, in my case, the experience barely lasted a year. I was engaged to be married. At the time, even for Protestants, the exercise of pastoral ministry by a married woman was judged as totally inappropriate.

Already engaged in my theological work, I hoped to follow it as a lay Orthodox theologian, married, pursuing it within the royal priesthood to which all who are baptized are called. Even so, it was not without heartache that I left my parishioners. We have kept up friendly relations for a long time. From this experience I keep the memory of a time of grace and, pinned to my heart, the hope that one day women, responding to new needs, will be able to exercise a ministry analogous to mine—whatever the title may be—in the heart of the Orthodox Church.

NOTES

1. For reasons of history, the Lutheran Church of Alsace-Lorraine benefited from a particular situation within French Protestantism, namely that it was a concordat-church, one officially recognized by the state.

2. Fr Lev Gillet, the first translator of Fr Sergius Bulgakov's important work *The Orthodox Church* into French in 1932, rendered Khomiakov's term *sobornost* by "symphonicity."

3. See my biography, *Lev Gillet, Un moine de l'Église d'Orient* (Paris: Cerf, 1993). [Editor's note: now translated by Helen Wright, *Lev Gillet, A Monk of the Eastern Church* (Oxford: Fellowship of St Alban and St Sergius, 1999).]

2

Orthodox Theological
Formation in the 21st Century:
The Tasks Involved*

May I first of all say what a great joy it is for me to be among you in the setting of Cambridge University, a place associated for me with a wonderful and very musical stay at St John's College a considerable time ago, when one of my English grandsons was a choral scholar in that famous choir. Thank you most especially for giving me, along with your invitation, a part in this event which, as I see it, constitutes the founding of an institute for the study of Orthodox Christianity within this ancient and eminent University of Cambridge, at the heart of western intellectual life.

This project, this founding that is in the process of becoming a reality, thanks to the University's theological teaching and also to the close collaboration between those appointed by the various Orthodox communities in Great Britain and representatives from Cambridge University, is a response to pastoral concerns. The multi-ethnic Orthodox communities that are becoming more and more firmly rooted in the United Kingdom must, if they are to be true sources of the spiritual life, have a clergy and a laity that have received solid theological formation. They will, in the future, be able to receive this formation here, on the spot, instead of having to look for it abroad, with the various inconveniences that it involves, including high costs and the risk of difficulty in adapting to the local culture. This is important. However, the full significance of the opening here in Cambridge of an institute for the study of Orthodox Christianity, while providing for these local pastoral needs, goes much further. As with the founding with very few resources of the Institute of Orthodox Theology of St Sergius in Paris in 1925, this new founding comes in the wake of a fruitful and—we use

---

* Adapted from a talk given at the Orthodox Theological Institute at St David's College, Cambridge University, December 12, 1998.

the word as believers—providential encounter of the Christian East and the Christian West, an encounter for which the worldwide Orthodox diaspora in the twentieth century has provided a ready ground, the *kairos* as the Greeks put it, the grace offered by the Lord of history.

The historical context of today's founding is very different from that of 1925. The latter was made possible by the presence in Paris of avant-garde Russian religious thinkers who had been driven from their homeland by the Bolshevik revolution, men and women whose eyes remained nostalgically turned toward Russia. Today, three-quarters of a century later, the communist regimes of eastern Europe have collapsed, and at the heart of a global and multifarious Orthodox *diaspora* we are witnesses of the emergence of an Orthodoxy that is western in culture, tentative and confronted with many obstacles though it may still be. However, a common vocation to witness to Orthodoxy in the West, together with a growing awareness of the universality of true Orthodoxy, creates very deep bonds of solidarity between the St Sergius Institute in Paris and this institute that is in process of creation here at Cambridge. It is in his awareness of this solidarity of destiny and vocation that Fr Boris Bobrinskoy, the dean of St Sergius Institute, asks me to convey to you his fraternal greetings and best wishes for the realization of your project. It was also on his friendly insistence that I have had the temerity to accept your invitation to speak—I, an old woman who has never held an office or professorship in Orthodox theology—about the tasks involved in Orthodox theological formation in the twenty-first century.

A preliminary question: the wording of the theme of this paper of mine could well risk provoking surprise, and even suspicion, from some of our Orthodox brothers and sisters. Could it establish an unwarranted relationship between the deposit of divine revelation, of eternal truth confided to the Church, and the passing of time? Does the Church's teaching change; is it called upon to change with the centuries? The task of Orthodox theological teaching in the twenty-first century, as in the preceding centuries, is the faithful transmission of the faith of the apostles, as expounded by those with the title Fathers of the Church and given its dogmatic form by the ecumenical councils. Could we have the sacrilegious presumption to change anything, as though it were ephemeral? Divine truth transcends time. The letter to the Hebrews proclaims "Jesus Christ, the same yesterday, today and forever" (13:8). And the apostle Paul exhorts the Christians "not to be like children tossed to and fro by every wind of doctrine" (4:14).

The disquiet that is expressed in this questioning must be taken seriously. We know of the book-burning that recently took place in Russia.[1] But it is based on a huge and disastrous misunderstanding, due precisely to a lack of theological formation. It is the turning of Christianity, of Christian truth, into a "system," a kind of "popular Platonism," as its critics call it, a world of ideas that, confined in its own eternity, hovers over the tragic history of the human race without ever becoming involved in it. This is not the living God of the Judaeo-Christian revelation, the God of Abraham, Isaac, Jacob, and Jesus Christ, who goes with his people as they cross the deserts, who speaks within history through the prophets, who becomes man in Jesus Christ, born of a woman during the reign of Caesar Augustus, crucified by the order of Pontius Pilate, the Roman governor of Judaea, who dies and rises before the eyes of his disciples and who, ascending to his heavenly Father, has promised his disciples that he would send them the Spirit who would lead them (note the future tense) into all truth (Jn 16:13). The fullness of this catholic and inexhaustible truth is, for Christ's disciples, Christ himself in person, revealing himself as the way, the truth, and the life (Jn 14:6). Christ, the word of God made flesh, with whom we are linked by the Spirit, the breath of Trinitarian love who proceeds from the Father, sustains in hope the whole of creation that is still groaning and travailing in the pain of being born, and waiting for deliverance when "God will be all in all" (Rom 8:22, 1 Cor 15:28).

Imbued with this hope, a hope that gives meaning to the history of humanity and consequently to every human being, we must examine the "signs of the times" as the Lord exhorts us (Mt 16:2-3) and, being attentive to the divine call that makes itself heard from within them, try to glimpse the tasks assigned to Orthodox theological formation in the twenty-first century.

What are these tasks? It goes without saying that in replying to this question, I can only throw out several ideas, sketch out certain propositions, which the discussion that is to follow this modest introduction must develop to full and right conclusions.

The task of Orthodox theological formation, it seems to me, is both ever the same and yet always new, always being renewed. It consists in the faithful transmission (an action not "rational" but "intelligent," in the sense of being the "Eucharist of the mind"), of the evangelical *kerygma*, of the original apostolic message. To be living, this transmission, this Tradition (giving the term its active meaning) must, in fidelity to the original and fundamental message, attempt to find answers to the new questions asked of the Church in its new circumstances. The Fathers of the Church did this in their day, in bringing the Gospel that had first been proclaimed in Aramaic to Galilean fishermen to the intellectual elite of the Graeco-Roman world.

Today, on the threshold of the twenty-first century, this proclamation of the eternal Gospel is called to stand right in the current and dynamic of the significant event to which my prefatory words refer. This is the encounter (new both in its breadth and its depth, through the Orthodox *diaspora* that has been formed during the twentieth century) of an Orthodoxy that had become eastern or Byzantine as a result of various historic cataclysms, with the western Christian world and with a modernity which, although it has been grown on this western soil, is in process of becoming truly global. The Orthodox, being called to an awareness of the universality of true Orthodoxy, are still selective and ambivalent in their understanding of this encounter, as are also some western Christians. It is experienced in different ways by Orthodox people according to the geographical area in which they live and the cultural and political factors that influence them. Here in the Orthodox *diaspora* in western Europe, and also in North America and Australia, the encounter with the West is part of daily life. It is intrinsic to a network of family relationships, friendships, and intellectual contacts. More than this, it has its place with its tensions, its questionings, its sufferings, and its joys within each one of us. In different degrees, we are all of both East and West.

Elsewhere, in countries such as Greece that are traditionally Orthodox and have an Orthodox majority, this encounter has for a long time remained more peripheral, reserved for a cultured class and a limited circle of theologians. But the situation is changing rapidly today. With the churches of eastern Europe, such as the Russian Church, that are just beginning to emerge from the isolation imposed on them by a totalitarian, atheist regime, and are being suddenly and brutally exposed to the great western common market of religions, the encounter with western Christianity is often experienced and rejected as aggression. These cleavages, I believe, bring a specific responsibility for the Orthodox theologians of the *diaspora*. Are they not called to be bridge-builders between East and West, both of them present but at times in conflict within an Orthodoxy that is in the pains of new birth, finding again its universal vocation?

The neo-patristic movement that has contributed so strongly to the renewal of Orthodox theology in the second half of the twentieth century came into being within the *diaspora*. Prepared within the "reformed" Russian theological academies of the nineteenth century, this renewal took flesh through the encounter of small groups of young theologians of the Russian emigration with masters of western historical science, such as Etienne Gilson in France, who were attempting to revive medieval theology, especially that of Thomas Aquinas, and make it comprehensible in its own dynamic. It was in the lecture halls of the Paris Sorbonne, where we followed with passionate interest the presentations of our teacher, Etienne Gilson, that (and I can testify to this) the theological and patristic vocation of my friend Vladimir Lossky was born. It was vital to confront the budding, Aristotelian, rationalist, and essentialist neo-Thomism with the mystical and personalist theology that was expressed in the paradoxes of the Greek Fathers and their Byzantine successors. This came about thanks to a movement of "*ressourcement*," "return to the sources," of which the publication in 1944 in Paris—in the midst of the convulsions of World War II—of Vladimir Lossky's *The Mystical Theology of the Eastern Church* served as a signpost. Whatever was creative in this movement must be continued, moving beyond its aspects that were ossified by anti-western polemics or marked by an ahistorical, numb clinging to the past. Fidelity to the Church's Tradition, a return to the great theologians of the first centuries of the Church, has never been identified with ossified traditionalism. This has been clearly stated by the true actors and artisans of Orthodox patristic renewal such as Vladimir Lossky, Georges Florovsky and, in the next generation, John Meyendorff. While preparing for this meeting today, I reread certain of these texts and I shall give in to the desire to quote them, as they seem to me to be of such immediate significance.

"Dead traditionalism," writes Fr John Meyendorff,

> cannot be truly traditional. It is an essential characteristic of patristic theology that it was able to face the challenges of its own time while remaining consistent with the original apostolic Orthodox faith. Thus simply to *repeat* what the Fathers said is to be unfaithful to their spirit and to the intention embodied in their theology... True Tradition is always a *living* Tradition. It changes while remaining always the same. It changes because it faces different situations, not because its essential content is modified. This content is not an abstract proposition; it is the living Christ himself, who said, "I am the Truth."[2]

When we speak of a return to the sources, it is not a question of a return to the past, but of a permanence and a faithfulness to revelation. This revelation judges the past as the present or the future of both East and West. Vladimir Lossky affirms, "Tradition is the Church's critical spirit." And to quote Meyendorff once again,

> One of the most basic problems for theologians today is knowing how to discern between the holy Tradition of the Church...and the human traditions which express Revelation only imperfectly and, very often, which even oppose and obscure it.... the Orthodox must do a bit of rethinking and reflecting themselves. If the truth which they are conscious of possessing is really Catholic truth, it must of course be valid for all men, all times and all countries. It must be capable of supplying an answer to the very real problems raised by Western Christians during the centuries which have elapsed since the separation. It must face the challenge of the modern world. In order to make their message meaningful, the Orthodox must learn to live these problems *from inside*, not externally.... they must learn to discipline themselves spiritually; there must be an act of love as well as of humility. It is all too obvious that while the Church as a supernatural body always possesses the fullness of divine life and truth, individuals, groups, nations, and local churches fail to conform to this life and this truth in all respects. In this regard, what may be called historical Orthodoxy, that is, the various nations which formerly made up or still make up the Orthodox world, have much to ask forgiveness for. Granted their history has been a particularly tragic one. The Arab, Turkish, and Mongol invasions and the recent martyrdom occasioned by the Russian revolution have all been so many terrible disasters interrupting the course of the development of the East. External factors of this kind largely explain, perhaps, the present weakness of Eastern Christianity. But there are also other weaknesses for which the Orthodox have only themselves to blame, in particular, the bane of excessive nationalism which has resulted in the harmful isolation of Orthodox churches from each other."[3]

This is a strong warning, an appeal to the conversion of mind and heart together, launched by one of the greatest Orthodox theologians of our day. A promoter of patristic renewal, Fr John Meyendorff was fully aware of its importance and its benefits. At the same time, however, he assessed the risk, the temptation to make patristics sacrosanct in an undefined way that was devoid of any critical spirit toward the past. This is a temptation to which Orthodox too often succumb, and from which they can be saved by a solid combination of historical and theological formation. For all that, there is no question in Orthodox theology of following the path of a modernism that dilutes the divine mystery confided to the

Church. Orthodox theologians must develop the capacity to discern, in a spirit of freedom, humility, and brotherly love, "speaking the truth in love" (Eph 4:15), between authentic Tradition, the mystery that transcends history while illuminating it, and that which, in the empirical life of the Church, is only a residue, often acceptable but sometimes noxious (in that it occludes the essential), of a past that is over and gone. It is in the light of the mystery of Christ, freed from the dross that too often conceals it, a secret revealed by the Holy Spirit who is present in the Church and by his very presence renders it all the more secret, that the Orthodox theologian must, in all humility, know he is called to answer the questions posed by western modernity, questions which he finds within himself and recognizes as his own.

This is the task, a daunting task, a long and exacting task and one even impossible by human standards, for the accomplishment of which he can only implore the help of the Holy Spirit, the Spirit of truth and love, the Father's breath that rests upon the Son and on his body, the Church.

I come now to the different areas in which this urgent conversion to "that essential thing that illumines all things" and that impregnates theological formation could bear fruit blessed by God. I shall touch briefly on these, confining myself to several concise points.

The pastoral formation of future priests is naturally under consideration, a formation too often neglected when theology is seen as an exclusive area of culture reserved for certain specialists in ancient languages or confused with a timeless moral code. We must also consider ecumenical dialogue, a dialogue aimed at the restoration or the progressive awareness of that unity of faith which is a necessary condition of sacramental communion. It goes without saying that, in this perspective, the distinction between Christ's "one thing needful" (Lk 10:42) and expressions of faith that are influenced by the historical cultures in which they are lived is of the greatest importance. It is germane to the Orthodox church's dialogue, not only with the Roman Catholic Church and the churches born of the sixteenth-century Protestant Reformation— the Lutheran and Reformed churches and the Anglican communion— but also with the ancient Oriental, non-Chalcedonian churches, the so-called "Monophysite" or "Nestorian" churches, that an honest and rigorous historical and theological investigation has brought us today to the overcoming of misunderstandings that have, alas, lasted for 1500 years. It is also in the light of the central mystery of the Christian revelation that it is proper to place the vitally important Christian dialogue with Judaism, an area in which Archimandrite Lev Gillet, an Orthodox who was a great mystic and also a great theologian, has played the role (one that is too easily forgotten today) of precursor. I am thinking of his important work, *Communion in the Messiah*, published in Great Britain in 1942, which it might be well to republish and use for study in the context of Orthodox theological formation.

In the postscript of one of his latest books, *Rome Autrement*, the French Orthodox theologian Olivier Clément sees the great task of the churches in the coming years as "the overcoming of modernism from the inside." This would in his view imply both the necessity of "responding to evil's argument" and to "take on oneself, in a theological and spiritual way, the global unity of humanity." "Today," Clément writes, "freedom in thrall to modernism is subjected to an anguished self-questioning." Christianity is called to respond to the anguish of death and the meaninglessness of life that undergird a seeming frenzy of living, "with a humble offering of a meaning to life, through the witness of lives risen in Christ." It is essential, in this perspective, to respond to evil's argument, an argument fundamental to the atheism of today and tomorrow, by pondering the *kenosis*, the self-emptying love of God, the vision of "God suffering" evoked by Fr Lev Gillet, "the vision of a God whose omnipotence, his almighty love, is inseparable from his all-weakness." It is by death, as the Orthodox sing at Easter, that Christ has conquered death.

An awareness of global human solidarity is one of the marks of modernism, though this can still meet with resistance. Could not the task of Christian theology be "to deepen solidarity in communion," the certainty that there exists "one single man, one unique Adam who is constantly broken by our sins yet constantly restored in Christ, in whom we are all consubstantial," a certainty that must be incarnated in love and the humble service of our neighbor?

The task in which all this of which I have spoken is contained is the ongoing understanding and diffusion of the mystery of God, one in three persons, the mystery of the living God who is so utterly one that he bears in himself the reality, the heartbeat of the other. The task is to reveal, in this vision of the one-in-three, the basis and paradigm of all true human relationships. For God became man that man, created in his image, might become god, a personal being in communion, in the image of God who is himself communion. These are some of the points that are today of extreme urgency in our thinking about the faith.

I would add here one last point to be explored. It is a point that has held my heart, both as a woman and as an Orthodox theologian who has, ever since the beginning of her Christian vocation, been engaged in ecumenical dialogue. As my friend Metropolitan Anthony Bloom of Sourozh exhorts us, the Orthodox are called to take to heart a problem that has for a long time been thought not to concern them, the problem of women's participation in the pastoral, liturgical, and sacramental ministry exercised by certain people in the Church, with the gifts, the responsibility, and the moral authority that this ministry implies. We are well aware that this problem has become a stumbling block in ecumenical dialogue. Distinguishing the essential necessity, which is the recognition of woman as a human person equal to man, free and responsible, called and loved by God, from that which, in the social status of women, is of the cultural order, and therefore relative and modifiable, it is necessary to seek a solution, or various solutions, to this problem in the light of Orthodox theological anthropology, Orthodox soteriology, and a true Christian theology of the ministries, most especially the presbyteral or priestly ministry.

I have dared to finish my paper with this appeal to prudent and courageous, open and calm reflection on a concrete and serious question that is posed by our western brothers and sisters, a question that is, for the Orthodox, becoming an internal problem.

I am very much aware of the omissions and imperfections of this paper. Please excuse this very old woman, "the grandmother of western Orthodoxy," as some people tease me by saying.

NOTES

1. Trans. note: Elisabeth Behr-Sigel is referring to the 1998 burning of the writings of Alexander Schmemann, Nicolas Afanasiev, John Meyendorff, and Alexander Men in the seminary of Ekaterinburg, with the approval of its then—now deposed—bishop Nikon.

2. John Meyendorff, *Living Tradition* (Crestwood, NY: St Vladimir's Seminary Press, 1978), pp. 7-8.

3. Meyendorff, *The Orthodox Church: Its Past and Its Role in the World Today*, 4th ed., rev. Nicolas Lossky (Crestwood, NY: St Vladimir's Seminary Press, 1996), pp. x-xi, 208-209.

3

Orthodoxy and Peace[*]

"In peace, let us pray to the Lord." This prayer opens the Orthodox eucharistic assembly. It follows another prayer which invokes the Spirit, "You who are everywhere, filling everything." The prayer for peace, for the highest messianic gift, the fullness of life, a foretaste of the kingdom of God which comes and which is already here in Jesus Christ, is at the heart of Orthodox prayer. Christ is celebrated as the "prince of peace" (Is 9:6), as the "rising star come from on high toward people who are in the shadows and the darkness of death to guide our feet along the path of peace" (Lk 1:79).

The great litany at the beginning of the eucharistic liturgy gathers all the intentions of this prayer: "For peace from on high and the salvation of our souls, for peace throughout the world, for the well-being of the holy churches and for the union of all... for the clergy and all the faithful... for the sick, the prisoners, for all those who are suffering... for peaceful times and abundance of the fruits of the earth, let us pray to the Lord." It is a prayer for the reconciliation of humanity with God, of every person with his neighbor, divine peace reaching out to the whole cosmos, to our relationship with the earth that we are called to cultivate and which in turn provides us with our food.

Greeting his disciples, the resurrected Christ proclaims, "Peace be with you." In the same way, the Orthodox priest, at the most solemn moments of the liturgy, addresses the faithful, proclaiming: "Peace be with you all." As the exchange of the kiss of peace by the celebrants signifies, it is only in a spirit of peace and mutual love that it is possible to confess the common faith and to draw near, "without judgment and condemnation," to the mystery of communion in the body given and the blood spilt by Christ for all people. The Eucharist is "a mystery of peace," emphasized St John Chrysostom.

* First published in *In Communion*, no. 3, Nativity Fast 1995, by the Orthodox Peace Fellowship at www.incommunion.org. Translated by Rachel Mortimer.

The great mystical prayer movement, which through the centuries has never ceased to vitalize Orthodox piety, carries the name hesychasm. *Hesychia* in Greek means rest or tranquillity. Of course it is not a matter of mere tranquillity of the spirit, of hardening of the heart, of spiritual sleep. The hesychast, in the assured abandon of faith, in Christ whose name, joined to one's breath, is in some way "breathed" unendingly, thereby strengthening communion in him to God united in three persons. Trinitarian love is the source, the paradigm of all human peace and communion. Far from encouraging lazy quietism, Orthodox mysticism calls one to spiritual combat: struggle, in the mysterious synergy of divine grace and human will which becomes aware of itself, in the face of selfish urges and "passions" which can destroy interior peace and peace in the world. The peace received from God can shine on the world through men and women who have experienced prolonged self-discipline or an enlightening event, living out peace and reconciliation. "Acquire peace and thousands around you will be saved," taught the great Russian mystic St Seraphim of Sarov (1759-1833). The monks' movement, hesychasm, and "the prayer of the heart" associated with it, underwent a significant diffusion among the Orthodox laity, as the famous work *The Way of the Pilgrim* testifies.

Nevertheless, different questions are raised: does the priority given to interior pacification not lead to the temptation of a certain dualism? Does it not serve as an excuse for resigned acceptance of, indeed compliance with, so-called "exterior" violence: the inevitable catch, existence in a world to which the Christian declares himself a stranger but to whose laws, hypocritically or cowardly, he submits himself? The historical Orthodox churches, along with other churches, have blessed armies that go to war. The deep links that have been forged between them and nations, in which the churches have sometimes played the role of midwife to the nations, enriching their culture, do these links not tend to degenerate into nationalism tinted with religiosity which justify warring conflicts? Orthodox believers must examine their own consciences at this point. An honest, historical inquiry could be a useful tool, as the perceptive theologian and historian Fr John Meyendorff has written. A simple allusion will have to suffice here.

The Orthodox Church has not worked out a theory or ideology of the "just war" or "holy war" and has abstained from preaching in support of crusades. She maintains her place in the continuity of the Church of the first centuries, which opposed her violent persecutors by means of the powerful gentleness of the martyrs. In the beatitudes sung at each Sunday liturgy, she proclaims, "Blessed are the meek, for they shall inherit the earth," namely the eschatological kingdom. Nevertheless, seen in a historical context, the Church (which lives on through the Orthodox Church) finished by admitting that war, in certain circumstances, could constitute a lesser evil. She no longer condemned carrying weapons as incompatible with the Christian faith.

A marked turning point was reached in the Constantinian era with the institution not of Caesaropapism (of which the church of Byzantium was wrongly accused) but with the arrival of the idea of the utopia of the "Christian empire," the empire seen as the temporal home of the Church, called to protect and defend the "true faith." The emperors saw this cementing of the unity of the state as a multicultural act. The teaching of the Orthodox faith belonged to the Church. The state, whose legitimacy the Church admits, believed it has to impose it by a coercion which, alas, she sometimes invoked: a fatal error, largely responsible—as it is recognized nowadays—for the disastrous schism which separated the imperial church from the ancient, eastern, non-Chalcedonian churches, wrongly called on the one hand "Nestorians" and on the other, "Monophysites."

Born out of the missionary growth of the church of Byzantium, the new Christians, who settled in the Balkans and at the eastern confines of Europe at the dawning of the Middle Ages, inherited the idea and thinking from the Christian empire, adapting it to new and different historical contexts.

The formation of the Russian state, first Kievan and then Muscovite, bears the mark of this influence. In the thirteenth century, Kievan Orthodox Russia suffered devastating raids by the "heathen" or Islamicized people of the steppes in the East and South while there was growing pressure in the West from the Teutonic knights (missionaries armed with Latin Catholicism). The Church, protector of the nations, was seen as guarding the unity of the Russian people. In the following century, St Sergius of Radonezh, a great monk from northern Russia, urged the rival Russian princes to gather outside Moscow in order to chase off the Tartars. After the fall of Constantinople in 1453, the myth of "Moscow, the third Rome" was born and spread through Russian monastic communities. At first with a hint of apocalypticism, it developed into the idea of Russia's vocation as a great imperial, if not imperialistic, power.

In the eighteenth century, the reforms of Peter the Great transformed the now headless Russian Church—she no longer had a patriarch—into an imperial administrative department. However, paradoxically, the secularized Russian state set itself up as protector, first of all to Orthodox subjects in the Ottoman Empire, then to Orthodox states born out of the dislocation of this empire, a pretension which justified many wars. Again in 1914, Czar Nicholas II, with great hesitation, believed himself obliged to declare war on Catholic Austro-Hungary, which was threatening Orthodox Serbia.

However, at the very interior of the Russian Church, an evangelical current, personalist, universalist, and mystical—a current which was persecuted by the official church and therefore often underground—did not cease rising up against the conscription of the Church by the state. It was represented in the fifteenth century by St Nilus of Sora, promoter of Russian hesychasm, whose disciples refused to associate themselves with the hunting down of heretics called "Judaizers"; by St Philip, Metropolitan of Moscow, assassinated upon the order of Ivan the Terrible, for daring to protest; and later by the daring "fools for Christ" from the sixteenth and seventeenth centuries that an English traveler compared to the "lampoonists" in his own country. Although officially condemned, Tolstoyism perhaps constituted one of the manifestations of this evangelical protest, a concept which is also expressed by a humble monk, the Archimandrite Spiridon, author of *My Missions in Siberia*.

Deep ties between Balkan peoples—Greeks, Bulgarians, Serbs, Romanians—and the Orthodox Church have become knotted up during a long and tragic history. After the fall of Constantinople, after the disappearance of the short-lived Serbian and Bulgarian kingdoms and the battles lost, like that of Kosovo whose mythical memory the Serbs preserve, these people lived for centuries under Ottoman domination, sometimes Austro-Hungarian. It is the Church that, through the Christian faith transmitted essentially by the liturgy celebrated in a tongue close to the vernacular, allowed them to preserve the essence of their local culture.

Orthodoxy was not, however, a permanent foyer of insurrection during this period. The Ecumenical Patriarch of Constantinople, on whom the local Orthodox churches depended canonically, put up with the regime which was both protective and restrictive of the *millet* given by Islam to the "Christian people" whose patriarch became the head of both civil and religious affairs. It is only at the end of the eighteenth century and at the beginning of the nineteenth that Orthodoxy truly became, according to the expression of Olivier Clément, "the fertile product of the nations' development" in the Balkans. This occurred, partly, under the influence of ideas originating in the West: from the French Revolution and from German romanticism. It was an Orthodox prelate, archbishop of Patras, who, raising the standard of revolt, called the Greeks to combat "for faith and the fatherland" in 1821. From the victorious insurrection came forth both modern Greece and the autocephalous church of Greece. In the last century, other Balkan races reached the same independence by similar means, though not without intervention by foreign powers. This independence was crowned by obtaining the sometimes difficult auton-omy of their "national" churches, which was not without ill effect. The patriarchate of Constantinople obtained the censure of phyletism from the assembly of Orthodox churches called to council in 1872. Phyletism, literally love of the tribe, was condemned as an "introduction of national rivalries within the Church of Christ."

It still exists today, after two world wars which have created more vic-tims in traditionally Orthodox countries of eastern and southeastern Europe than elsewhere, after decades of atheist, communist regimes that aimed at cutting the ties between people, the nations, and the Church. Consequently the Orthodox Church has undergone a geographical frag-mentation following various political cataclysms. In the light of these events, what is the attitude of the Orthodox churches confronting efforts to promote international peace? It must be recognized that the picture is a contrasting one. I must content myself with summary information.

Primus inter pares, first among equals, the Ecumenical Patriarch of Con-stantinople, as the title indicates, has a supranational vocation and appears agreeable to peace initiatives, whether from the Vatican or the World Coun-cil of Churches. (He has only a small number of faithful in Turkey itself, where the very existence of the patriarchate is under threat.) This attitude was found among the ancient patriarchs of Antioch and Alexandria, whose role was important within the Council of Christian Churches in the Middle East, as well as in the context of Islamic-Christian dialogue. Prompted by Arab solidarity, these churches appear more reserved with regard to the state of Israel. The Church of Greece, on the other hand, feels called to defend Christian Hellenism against an Islam which asserts itself in Turkey and also in Cyprus and, it thinks, in the Balkans.

The great and tumultuous Russian Church is crossed by conflicting currents, some characterized by a national identity withdrawal, others open to the positive values of the West: democracy, tolerance, and respect for human rights. The Patriarch of Moscow, Alexis II, himself remains well anchored in the World Council of Churches,[1] participating through such representatives as Metropolitan Kyrill of Smolensk in the movement for "Peace, Justice, and the Integrity of Creation." Patriarch Aleksii has condemned the war in Chechnya.

Among the dispersed Orthodox communities, some remain very attached to the national churches from which they came and are therefore threatened, on the lookout for nationalist reactions. But others in Europe and America are integrated into western culture. Enriched by the thought of the great theologians from the Russian emigration, the Orthodox *diaspora* has been the place in the twentieth century for a powerful awareness of the spiritual catholic heritage of the Orthodox Church, in the sense of symphonic universality. This movement is nowadays taken over by Orthodox theologians of differing ethnic origins who, by a creative return to the sources, to Scripture and the Fathers, aspire to the liberation of national orthodoxies. One of the greatest contemporary Orthodox theologians, Archimandrite Lev Gillet, was a pioneer of ecumenical dialogue, Judaeo-Christian dialogue as well as inter-Christian dialogue. His reflections and prophetic messages play a growing role within Orthodoxy.

We cannot talk about Orthodoxy in relation to the ideal of peace between nations, Church and state, without calling to mind the tragedy of former Yugoslavia. In their judgment of this disastrous conflict, the western media and intellectuals are often proof of the ignorance of the complex and sorrowful history of the people concerned. It would not be a matter of justifying the horrors committed by some Serbs today in the name of the suffering inflicted on the Serbian people in the past—the genocide committed by the Croat Ustashi, and before that the tyrannous demands of the Ottoman period. But it would seem rash to ask the Serbs simply to forget. As Mara Dropovitch has written, true reconciliation will be the fruit, not of a forgotten past, but of its incorporation in a spirit of penitence and mutual forgiveness. All churches can and should contribute to this difficult process of purification of the memory. The Serbian Orthodox Church today appears ready to follow this route. It has broken solidarity not with its people who are also suffering but with the ambiguous politics of Milosevic. "Evil and hatred create only new evil and hatred," Patriarch Pavle declared last May. "If this war proceeds, the only victors will be the devil and evil, not peoples and nations."

An Orthodox peace movement, called the Orthodox Peace Fellowship, has been born in recent years and is gradually becoming more active. It has members in Serbia as in many other countries. May the God of peace defeat the powers of darkness and division!

NOTES

1. Ed. note: This article was written before the recent tumultuous events in the World Council of Churches provoked a so-far temporary withdrawal on the part of the patriarchate of Moscow and also before the start of the second war in Chechnya, this time fully endorsed by Patriarch Alexei of Moscow.

4

The Kenotic, the
Humble Christ*

In his epistle to the Christians at Philippi, the apostle Paul wrote: "Have this mind among yourselves which is yours in Christ Jesus, who though he was in the form of God did not count equality with God a thing to be grasped, but emptied himself, taking the form of a servant, being born in the likeness of men" (Phil 2:5-7). When it is used in reference to this text, the term *kenosis* belongs to both a spiritual and a technical theological vocabulary. Kenotic spirituality and theology are often considered more characteristic of western than of eastern Christianity. The majestic Christ Pantocrator of the Byzantine churches along with certain aspects of patristic christology are more often associated with eastern Christianity. Orthodoxy, with its central vision of the divine *Logos*, including within its radiance the humble humanity of Jesus of Nazareth, becomes erroneously associated with eastern Christians. Such a dichotomy seems to be rather superficial. It ignores the many riches of historical Orthodoxy and the interior balance of the ecclesial vision (in which Antioch counterbalanced Alexandria) contemplating Christ in the depths of his humanity just as in his divinity.

Throughout Orthodox theology, the theme of *kenosis* is given particular attention in Russian spirituality. Russia is situated at the juncture of eastern and western Christianity, a fact that is more spiritual than geographic. The soul of the Russian people, deeply touched even in its collective unconscious by the Orthodox faith, knows how to sing in an incomparable manner the cosmic joy of the resurrection. At the same time the Russian people can hear the voice of the master of the beatitudes and contemplate the "man of sorrows," the Lamb of God offered for the sins of the world.[1]

* First published in the journal *La table ronde*, no. 250, November 1968, pp. 204-217, later re-edited for *Cahiers Saint Dominique*, no. 170, December 1977, and published most recently in the 1982 Cerf edition of *Prière et sainteté dans l'Église russe*, originally published in 1950. Translated by Lyn Breck.

Russian piety, then, is marked by two different yet complementary aspects: on the one hand, there is the experience of actual participation in the resurrection, that luminous vision of the world transfigured "in hope," already on the path of transfiguration; and on the other hand, there is the tender suffering of the passion and the cross of Jesus which extends to the suffering of all mankind. While these differing aspects of spirituality can be attributed to national temperament, we must also recognize a profound charismatic intuition of the heart converted by grace: spiritual intelligence crucified yet capable of recognizing the divine absolute as a gift and sacrifice. The suffering and humiliated humanity of the Russian people became mysteriously radiant in Christ Jesus.

After a long period of silence, Christian Russia began to find its voice again in the great creators of Russian culture during the nineteenth century. Nadejda Gorodetzky,[2] a historian of modern Russian thought, discovered the theme of *kenosis* as an essential thread. The topic of the humiliated Christ appeared in the works of novelists, poets, and journalists, whether they were western or eastern, believers or nonbelievers, faithful of the Orthodox Church or antagonists. At times this topic could be clearly deciphered. At other times it was obscured by foreign ideologies. It was, however, always present.

To fully understand this phenomenon, it is important to explore Russian culture in order to discover the vestiges of a first encounter that was never forgotten. This unique and ever-present encounter, hidden in the depths of the collective memory, is none other than the encounter with the Christ of the Gospels. At the inception of the nation, despite its history of sin, this encounter with Christ influenced the spiritual destiny of Russia.

Christian Russia

It is known how Russia was evangelized during the tenth century by Byzantium, receiving the Christian faith through the spiritual treasure of the Gospel and the eastern liturgy. Both were translated into the native tongue. Christian Russia, being a humble and gentle student of the great Church, became conscious of its identity through this process of assimilation. Few documents have survived to this time. We are left with only a partial understanding of the soul of this obscure period of history. However, by the nineteenth century, there were manuscripts of popular songs and very old "lives of saints" that had been copied from one generation to the next. These documents seemed to be a naive and hesitant expression of the Christian ideal of holy Russia. For even more than the historic event that had inspired them, these lives of saints focused on a certain idea of Christian holiness through which the Russian people had internalized the image of Christ.

Three types of saints are significant: the *strastoterpets* or suffering one, the *iurodivyi* or fool for Christ, and the *starets* or typical monastic ideal. All three, in different ways, reveal a deliberate choice of the path of humility and sacrificial love, illumined by the Son of God.[3] All three are unique to Russian hagiography as compared to other models of holiness inherited from Byzantium or from ancient Christianity.

For the Russian people, a *strastoterpets* is "one who suffers the passion" as Christ suffered. Prototypes of this path to sanctity are the young princes Boris and Gleb who were assassinated in 1015 by their older brother Sviatopolk. By 1029 the Russian people clamored for their recognition as saints while the ecclesiastical authorities wavered. Their canonization was the first in Russia. These two princes were not martyrs in the strict sense of confessors of the Christian faith. Rather their humanity is emphasized. Young and handsome, they begged their captors to spare them so as not to have to leave "the wonderful light." "Have mercy on my youth, Lord," Gleb cried to his killer, "you will be my lord and I will be your slave." Boris also cried out, "Have mercy on my beautiful body." Both, however, having sent away the soldiers who could have defended them, did not resist their murderers. Allowing their throats to be slit "as lambs at the slaughter," they forgave their enemies and entered into the presence of Christ. "Lord Jesus," Boris prayed, "thou who didst voluntarily allow thyself to be nailed to the cross and to suffer the passion for our sins, allow me to suffer my passion... which I receive not from the hands of enemies but from the hand of my brother. Forgive him."

During the time of the Tartars, the princes who defended their town and people from the Khan and the hordes were also venerated as *strastoterpetsy*. Other "suffering servants" for whom Russia had a strange veneration were the peasants, the simple-minded, the merchants, and innocent dead children. Metropolitan Philip of Moscow, who was strangled by the order of Ivan the Terrible, was also venerated as a *strastoterpets*. Even though these *strastoterpetsy* were quite different in social class, age, and the circumstances of their deaths, they all had one thing in common. All seemed to be innocent victims who offered no resistance. In them, the Russian people recognized the "lamb of God slain for the sins of the world." Grafted onto their sacrifice, the death of these innocents was a victory over death: miracles occurred at the site of their tombs and para-doxically, according to popular legend, these "pacifists" became celestial leaders and protectors of Russia against its enemies. The cross of Christ, symbol of all the suffering ones, became in them as well a sign of triumph.

Another category of saints, the fools for Christ's sake, if not entirely Russian at least was less recognized elsewhere. Interpreting to the letter the first beatitude according to St Matthew, "Blessed are the poor in spirit," with reference also to the Pauline preaching in regard to the folly of the cross, ancient Russia venerated as saints people who feigned simple-mindedness. Some actually were mentally ill. In the sixteenth century, several fools for Christ's sake such as Basil the Blessed (in whose memory the cathedral of the Kremlin was built by Ivan the Terrible) took on the role of prophet in the heart of the Russian state church. Protected in some measure by their ascetic rigor and by popular veneration, they dared to denounce the cruelty of the czars and the pharisaism of the ruling class, often with holy humor or simply a crazy boldness. This approach contrasted greatly with the typical submission of the hierarchs to the state church. Weakened and humiliated in their ability to reason, the fools appeared to the powerful as the image of God's mysterious wisdom, "despised and crucified by the princes of the world, power of God for believers" (1 Cor 1-2).

Frequently suspect and often persecuted by the official church, these fools for Christ's sake survived in Russia through the nineteenth century to the dawn of the twentieth century in the person of the pilgrim, simple of mind, straying from place to place. Such is the innocent Grisha described by Leo Tolstoy in his work *Childhood*, surprised by a group of children while saying his bedtime prayers. Thirsting for opportunities for self-humiliation, the fools for Christ seemed at the same time to be filled with love and joy. One of them is said to have died whispering, "Be saved! May the whole earth be saved."[4] Considering their saintly image and their profound sense of direction, one can see in the fools for Christ a reflection of God's insane love even to the victorious folly of the cross.

The *starets*, for Russians, was their ideal holy monk.[5] Zosima of *The Brothers Karamazov*, who typified the *starets*, has become known through world literature. This type of holy person is not unique in Russia. The Greek *pater pneumatikos*, emanating from the desert tradition of early Christianity, corresponds to the *starets* in Russia. The originality of the Russian *startchestvo* lies in the tendency to broaden and deepen the notion of spiritual fatherhood while simultaneously viewing it as the highest form of solitary contemplation and angelic service of the monk. Called to seek God in the desert, whether it be in the solitude of the Kievan caves or in the impenetrable forests of central Russia, the greatest Russian monastics were always discovered by the people. Thus the nuptial union of the soul with the Lord was realized in charitable action.

So the Son of God urges them to descend from their angelic, contemplative dwellings toward their brethren on earth. St Sergius of Radonezh, who loved silence and founded the movement of hermit monks in the fourteenth century, renounced his solitary life to take over the direction of a substantial monastic community. St Nilus of Sora, who practiced the "prayer of the heart" and dwelt in a skete with two or three other monks, welcomed guests and accepted being "insane for the love of his brothers." After a whole life spent in solitude and years of silence, St Seraphim of Sarov opened wide the door of his monastic cell to receive vast numbers of visitors. He would greet each one with the words, "My joy!" As for the *startsy* of the Optino monastery, they denied their "selves," practicing a kind of self-abasement in a deep bowing before each person who approached them. This symbolic act expressed the renouncement of self. *Starets* Ambrose said, "I have spent my time patching the roofs of others while my own still has many holes." And so this solitary path of hesychasm and the prayer of the heart through the invocation of Jesus' name comes to fruition in the communion in Christ of all who are burdened.

Tikhon of Zadonsk

Generally speaking, the eighteenth century was a period of spiritual decadence for the Russian Church. The "old believers" began leaving the Church in the seventeenth century due to a rupture caused by two monastic tendencies. One group, represented by Joseph of Volokholamsk, espoused the accumulation of property and estates. Nilus of Sora defended the contemplative path that embraced absolute poverty for monks.

Tikhon of Zadonsk appeared alone yet prophetically significant. He was the historical prototype of *Starets* Zosima in Dostoevsky's novel, *The Brothers Karamazov*. Tikhon was a theologian who proclaimed the Pauline preaching of the cross while at the same time being a mystic and a moralist, applying his vision of the kenotic Christ to individuals and society. As a young bishop, he was more burdened by intellectual exercises than by administrative tasks. He was in charge of the very poor diocese of Voronezh where he was deeply touched to discover the face of the humble Christ in the serfs exploited by landowners, in his own ignorant and miserable clergy, in all the people both rich and poor who were plunged into spiritual darkness. This recluse of Zadonsk (he withdrew to the monastery there) was a theological and spiritual man who meditated without ceasing on the kenotic verses of Philippians 2; "the condescension of the Son accepted of his own free will with the cooperation of the Holy Spirit" was for him the "source of all grace." He would delve into the mystery of this humiliation not to fathom it intellectually but to search out the paradoxes: Christ dwelt among men but without being separated from the bosom of the Father (Jn 1:18). He took upon himself the condition of a slave (Phil 2:7) but as Lord he commanded floods and storms.

Ultimately Tikhon applied his theology of *kenosis* to practical questions both moral and spiritual. In his sermons and writings, he boldly reminded Christians, particularly the privileged classes, of the implication of this doctrine of life: "The Son of God humiliated himself and you, can you be filled with pride? He took the condition of a slave and you, can you wish to be in command? He was poor and you, you desire wealth? He was scorned and you, you aspire to honors? He washed the feet of his disciples and you, you would find it shameful to serve your neighbor?"

Toward Humility

In all scientific, literary and artistic areas, the nineteenth century is characterized by Russia's access to the circles of high European culture. In this context, Russia feels obliged to make a comment. Brothers who can't abide each other, supporters of both the East and the West, those embracing popular religion, and revolutionary nihilists, all alike are filled with a love for the great people of Russia. Paradoxically, it is their humility which is so attractive. For committed Christians, these humble people are great because they carry the image of Christ within. For others who have given up their childhood faith, this Messiah people becomes a kind of substitute for Christ.

> O these miserable villages
> O this indigent nature
> Land of long suffering!
> Land of our Russian people!
>
> Burdened by the weight of the cross,
> The king of Heaven, as a humble slave,

Has journeyed through your mother country
From one end to another, blessing you.

Not without a certain ambiguity, these few verses of Tioutchev express the essence of the love of Russia. Nekrasov, a liberal westernizer and singer of Russia's anger and shame, speaks not only with compassion but also with admiration of those

Who tolerate all in the name of Christ
Whose eyes do not shed tears
The silent lips whisper no longer
Who work with their rough hewn hands
Respectfully allow us
To plunge ourselves into the arts and sciences
Giving ourselves over to dreams and passions.

In answer to this poet's call, "Go toward the humble, reach out to those with bruised hearts," thousands of young Russians of the privileged classes committed themselves to a kenotic way of life. This meant that they took the path of "descent toward the people" to "pay their debt" and assuage their consciences. "To remain in a privileged position, even a modest one, was considered a betrayal," wrote the atheist Larov. "It was untenable to be freed from the obligation to share the sufferings of the people."

Throughout Literature

Without a doubt this revolutionary kenosis, which was inspired by a purely human image of Christ, was doctrinally suspect. However, one cannot deny its basic Christian roots. It would be even less possible to discuss Russian spirituality without turning to the literature from Gogol to Dostoevsky (leaving behind the classicism of Pushkin, where we note the dramatic confrontation between man and God).

Ivan Turgenev, essentially a pessimist, gladly presented himself as a liberal Westernizer. In his *Sketches from a Hunter's Album*, he nevertheless developed characters who express with strength and justice a conception of life and death inspired by the traditional faith of the Russian people. There is Akhim, ruined by his wife's lover, and the young Lukeria in the story "Living Relics" who, paralyzed by an accident, accepts her lot with the resignation of a saint. In one of his "Poems in Prose," Turgenev tells how one day in a village church he had a vision of Christ. This Christ had the face of a peasant, "a face like all the others."

While the work of Turgenev is etched in the faith of others he understands without sharing their faith, the entire painful and tormented existence of Nikolai Gogol witnesses to his attempt to live out his faith. A splendid writer, Gogol claims that only art can justify life. In a moment of folly, he burned the second part of *Dead Souls*, a work which took him five years to complete, a work into which he poured the best of himself. "If the grain of wheat does not die," he writes on this subject, "one must die for there to be resurrection."

The Christ of whom Gogol speaks in his correspondence appears as the supreme judge before whom all men must be accountable. With his fiery look, he penetrates the hidden depths of the soul. Later in Gogol's *Meditation on the Divine Liturgy*, the poet refers to the appearance in the world of him "by whom the world was made... He did not appear in the form of unbridled imagination, with prideful power, as the avenger of transgressions, or a judge empowered to annihilate some and reward others. No."

Gogol's personal path was a kenotic one too. After publishing *Selected Passages from Correspondence with Friends*, he was the butt of the most unjust and violent attacks. He humbly accepted "public scourging." "Gathering as much courage as I could, given my weakness," he wrote, "I decided to tolerate everything for the sake of being able to practice relentless self-evaluation... As to my suffering, oh well, one must sacrifice something. I, also, need to be buffeted about in public and without a doubt I need it more than others."[6]

Through many excerpts from his writings, the religious leanings of Leo Tolstoy are well known. After his "conversion" to a Christianity based solely on the Gospels, he took a prophetic critical stance toward both the state and the Church. As he grew older, his rationalism became more rigid. He rejected all the traditional mysteries of the Church. His fiery alienation from the Orthodox Church made its mark. Frequently the religious writer Tolstoy is juxtaposed with Tolstoy the great epic novelist. Essentially, however, the same moral, practical question haunts him throughout his life. Nekhloudov in *Anna Karenina* (1873-1877) asks this question of Levine: "How can you live justly?" Another Nekhloudov in *The Resurrection* (1899) replies: "By considering yourself not as a master but rather as a servant." For Tolstoy, this is the essence of the Gospel which, he senses, is better understood by the poor than by those who are wealthy and well educated. The first condition necessary to acquire a new life is therefore to renounce all wealth, material and intellectual.

Tolstoy's doctrine of deism is certainly comparable to the naturalism of Rousseau. Kenotic theology, the humbling of the Son of God, held no meaning for him. But Tolstoy loved the Christ of the Gospels and remained forever attracted to him who said, "I am gentle and humble of heart." Perhaps the depths of his soul somehow remained Christian in spite of his heretical thoughts. Perhaps in these words his truth is revealed: "'Take my yoke upon you and learn from me...' I am not able to express what these words evoke in me or how much I find in them an answer to everything. No, this self, this prideful and stained self aspires to perfection. But accepting me as I am with my body, my health, my personality, my past, even my sin in the depths of my heart at each moment, in gentleness and humility, I desire to accomplish the work that he [Christ] expects of me."[7]

In his personality and convictions, in his way of life and his works, Fyodor Dostoevsky distinguished himself from Tolstoy. This is even more remarkable since his intuition about the essence of life is in fact quite close to Tolstoy's ideal. Just like Tolstoy, Dostoevsky experienced a conversion because of the Gospels of Christ. In *The Journal of a Writer* he tells of Von Vizine's wife who, upon her arrival in Siberia, offered Dostoevsky the gift of a small Gospel book which he kept under his pillow during the four years of his imprisonment. It was during these terrible years, when "he became thirsty for the faith" just like "dried-up grass," that he composed his "credo" or statement of faith: "To believe that there is nothing more beautiful, more profound, more perfect than Christ."[8] In *The House of the Dead*, the radiant face of this God-man saved him from despair. In the light of Christ, the roughhewn faces of his fellow inmates, many of whom were crude criminals, were illumined. Communion with them was possible.

The questions "What to do?" and "How to live?" remained. At the heart of Tolstoy's dilemma was the problem of faith, a faith of the past that passes through the hell of doubt. For Dostoevsky, these same questions recur in an existential rather than a theoretical context. In a world where innocent people suffer, how can one believe in God? In accepting his creation, how can God hold onto the insane project of freedom for man? Dostoevsky discovered that there were no answers to these questions other than Christ himself. In his fragile humanity without defense, he was delivered over to the oppressors of the Great Inquisitor. His burning kiss placed on the bloodless lips of the old man is a call freely to embrace faith and love.

Above all, Dostoevsky was an artist who did not elaborate on any theology of *kenosis*. The mystery of the incarnation, however, was for him the key to the universe. "Peace for mankind," says his character Stavrogin, "the source of life and salvation for all, deliverance from despair, the condition sine qua non of the existence of the universe, are included in these words: The Word became flesh." It seals the union of God with the flesh of man and with the flesh of the promised land of hope in giving birth to the children of God. This is the mystery of the tenderness of joy revealed, not to noble and strong souls, but through the valley of tears to the weak, the little ones as sinners aware of their unworthiness: "If you flood the earth with your tears, you will be joyful," stammered Stavrogin's infirm wife. Just as for Tolstoy, the path of salvation for Dostoevsky was a kenotic path. It was realized in kenotic humiliation, humility, and renouncing of self. Without a doubt, the common people are much closer to this kenotic path than the nobles and intellectuals. This pathway to humility for each person is not an interpersonal exercise; rather, it consists of each one descending into the hell of his own heart and there acknowledging his miserable condition as a sinner in order to receive the gift of tears which today will open the gates of paradise. When Stavrogin confided to the hermit his intention to publish his confession, the hermit said, "If only you could accept with humility the spitting and the blows! The most shameful cross could not fail to change the most sincere humility into power and glory. Even in this life you will be consoled."

We know that Dostoevsky was inspired by the biography of Tikhon of Zadonsk. He was also inspired by a personal encounter with the spiritual elders of Optino Monastery which led him to create the character of *Starets* Zosima. Generally speaking, we can find the same types of holy people in which we have seen the kenotic vision of old holy Russia portrayed in the modern characters of Dostoevsky's novels: Sonia of *Crime and Punishment*, the ailing wife of Stavrogin in *The Possessed*, Dimitri in *The Brothers Karamazov.* We see also the innocent victims, the *strastoterpetsy*, whose sins are pardoned as in the case of Dimitri by submitting to an unjust punishment. The innocent prince Myshkin of *The Idiot* seems to be a kind of fool for Christ's sake. In addition to these more traditional ways, we see sketched out in *The Brothers Karamazov*, Dostoevsky's last work and in some ways his last testament, an imprecise outline of the new kenotic path. On his deathbed, *Starets* Zosima mysteriously predicts to Alyosha whose face he loved to see, "You will leave these walls. You will dwell in the world as a monk... Life will bring you much pain but you will find there joy; you will bless it and persuade others to bless it, this is vital."

Feodor Bukharev

In composing those lines, was Dostoevsky thinking of the particular destiny of his contemporary, Archimandrite Feodor Bukharev? The fact is that in the life and work of this Archimandrite, the vocation of *starets* was the incarnate taking form in reality: the spiritual came down from the realm of the angelic dwellings of contemplation toward the temporal existence of mankind, taking on their burdens and their work in an effort to enlighten and save.

Bukharev was of very humble origins, the son of a poor village deacon. He was an excellent student at the Seminary of Tver, then at the Academy of Moscow, where he was noticed by the well-known Metropolitan Philaret. After his entrance into monastic life, he was taken on as professor at the Academy. Young Bukharev seemed to have a brilliant and promising career ahead of him, despite a few run-ins with the ecclesial authorities. Named to the ecclesiastical court in St Petersburg, in 1860 he published his work *Orthodoxy and the Modern World*, a book which caught on and seemed to deliver a "new word." This publication, however, was the cause of scurrilous attacks by the reactionary, bitter, and skeptical Askochensky. He was an editor of the weekly publication *Domashniaia Beseda* and presented himself as the defender of Orthodoxy, pitting the spirituality of Mt Athos against the pernicious influences of the modern world. Fearing a scandal, the ecclesial bureaucracy intervened, silencing Archimandrite Feodor and sending him to a monastery far away in the provinces.

Although Feodor obeyed, he filed a petition to be laicized, a decision which troubled many of his friends and furnished his adversaries with the necessary ammunition to treat him as a "new Luther," deploring his "moral fall." By Bukharev's own declarations, he stayed fully committed to the Church. He experienced the descent toward the world, with its resulting sacrifices and personal disgrace, as a kenotic path to which he felt called, following the example of Christ. Willing to live in the world as a "sinner who submits to penitence," he hoped to respond "with the wisdom of Christ who came down from the cross to our sinful world and appeared on the cross as the impersonation himself of sin and evil" (Gal 3:5; Col 5:21).

Bukharev's personal destiny was unique. But the theological intuition that was the foundation of his thought belongs to the Tradition of the Church. It is divine love, the creator and redeemer spread out upon the world and on each person in an immense gesture of tenderness and personal outpouring, of which the Word made flesh is the perfect revelation. Raising his eyes toward the Lamb slain for the sins of the world, Bukharev put all his hope of redemption and fulfillment of all that is human in Christ. On the eve of the revolution of 1917, the great Russian theologian Pavel Florensky published the correspondence of Bukharev. He affirmed that the true meaning of Bukharev's message "concerning the future" was yet to be understood. And so, according to Florensky, kenotic theology is called to found an authentic Christian humanism, without which the "innocent Feodor," in his prophetic yet often confused vision, could see none other than the ruin and destruction of mankind. Searching for "the signs of the times," Bukharev discovered the crisis of modern culture in its alienation from its spiritual roots. Conscious of this tragic rupture, he called all people of the Church to descend from the heights of the illusion of an unincarnate idealism and become conformed to Him who "truly assumed human nature except sin" according to the Spirit. He consciously took the step of becoming a monk in the world as a sign "in order to persevere," he said, "until the end of my life, to follow the Lamb of God and to reveal His light in all aspects of life."

Since then, once again, silence has fallen on Christian Russia. Can we not hope, nevertheless, that the image of the humble and victorious Christ, inscribed in its soul by the saints and prophets, will continue to console and strengthen by their longsuffering those who here continue to believe and pray?

NOTES

1. In a Rostov monastery that served as a museum, we saw a series of striking antique wooden sculptures of Jesus as the man of sorrows, seated and bent over under the weight of an invisible burden.

2. Nadejda Gorodetzky, *The Humiliated Christ in Modern Russian Thought* (London: Macmillan, 1938).

3. Ibid., *The Idea of Russian Holiness*, p. 27-74

4. D. Belenson, *The Fools for Christ's Sake*, in Russian (Pout: 1927).

5. See also Elisabeth Behr-Sigel, "Les Startsy russes," in *Concilium*, September 1968.

6. Nikolai Gogol, *Selected Passages from Correspondence with Friends* (Nashville, TN: Vanderbilt University Press, 1969). Letter to A. O. Rosetti.

7. Letters to V. V. Rakhmanov in *Oeuvres*, Birioukov Edition, vol. XXII, p. 61.

8. Letter to Madame Von Vizine, cited by C. Mochulskii. *Dostoevsky, Man and Works*, p. 125.

5

Mother Maria Skobtsova, 1891-1945[*]

A vant-garde poet in a refined intellectual milieu of St Petersburg, member of the Russian Socialist Revolutionary Party, twice married and divorced, mother of three children, then monastic in the heart of the Russian Church in exile, lastly member of the French Resistance, deported to Ravensbrück concentration camp where she died shortly before the liberation: such was the path of Mother Maria Skobtsova's life.[1]

Childhood and Family Life

Elisabeth Pilenko, the name of Mother Maria in the world, was born December 8, 1891, in Riga. Her family belonged to the Ukrainian landed noblemen. In the eighteenth century, one of her ancestors married Parascovie Romanov, the sister of Empress Anne of Russia. Elisabeth's father established a model vineyard on the family property near the town of Anapa on the shores of the Black Sea. It was there in a setting of sea and sun that Elisabeth spent a happy childhood which ended in tragedy when her father died prematurely.

This disturbed the turbulent adolescent to no end. Much later, Mother Maria spoke of this crisis: "The only thing which caused me distress was the crucial question to which there had to be an answer: Do I believe in God? Does God exist? Then came the answer: My father died. The thoughts which tumbled around in my head were very simple: This was an unjust death. There is no justice. And if there is no justice, then there is no just God. If there is no just God, then there is no God at all... I had discovered the adult's secret: God does not exist. The world is full of misery, pain, and injustice. And that was the end of my childhood."[2]

[*] First published in "Des Mères dans l'Église" from the course "Formation Oecumenique Interconfessionelle." Translated by Lyn Breck.

St Petersburg

At that time Elisabeth was fourteen years old. Shortly after the death of her father, she and her mother went to live in St Petersburg where the family had ties to those who were close to the imperial court.[3] But the young girl, who had already shown herself to be a talented poet, frequented the avant-garde literary circles of the time. The capital of imperial Russia was one of the centers of what was called the "Russian Religious Renaissance" at the beginning of the twentieth century.[4] Elisabeth took up with the symbolist poet, Alexander Blok. At the age of eighteen, she married Dmitrii Kuzmin-Karavaev,[5] a young lawyer, member of the Social Democratic Party. The young couple went out often. He was one of the refined elite who gathered in the "Tower" of the writer Viatcheslav Ivanov. This tower had a splendid view of the Douma Palace in Tauride Park.

The vanity of the discussions in this milieu turned out to be boring. They criticized the progressive intelligentsia for their interminably detailed discussions concerning the revolution while refusing to act and give their lives for it. Elisabeth herself became involved in a mystical, messianic vision of the Russian common people. In 1913, she wrote: "I am for the earth, for the simple people of Russia... I reject the culture of the uprooted elite that has no soul." For Elisabeth as for Dostoevsky, the "Mother Earth" as the source of life was sacred. Christ, however, was at the horizon of her world. "The people need Christ," she wrote. At the same time a desire to deepen her knowledge of Orthodox Christianity welled up. She became one of the first women, if not *the* first, to obtain permission to enroll in courses at the Academy of Theology of St Petersburg as a day student. In the meantime, her marriage broke up. A divorce made the separation final.

Revolution and Civil War

When the Russian Revolution broke out, Elisabeth belonged to the Socialist Revolutionary Party, an idealistic party which blended, not without some confusion, the ideas of Russian populism, with its goals of justice and truth, and the ideals of western democracy. We know what happened and how the cynical realism of Lenin's Bolshevik party triumphed in Russia, eliminating the majority Socialist Revolutionary party of the first democratically elected assembly. Fleeing Bolshevism in January of 1918, Elisabeth went to the family property in Anapa. There she was elected member of the municipal town council and eventually became the mayor. This occurred under the difficult circumstances of civil war subsequent to the overthrow of the monarchy by the Soviets. In August of 1918, Anapa was occupied by the White Army. An independent government was established at Kouban. Accused of collaborating with the local Soviets, the young woman was brought before the military tribunal. She was given a symbolic sentence and set free.

One of the judges was a young officer named Daniel Skobtsov. He fell in love with Elisabeth, whom he called Lise, and married her. Two children were born of this marriage, Yuri and Anastasia. Without giving up her revolutionary socialist ideals, or perhaps even because of them, Elisabeth fully shared her husband's anti-Bolshevik stance. Daniel Skobtsov had become a member of a provisional Ukrainian government. The hazards of civil war separated Elisabeth and Daniel. After the defeat of the White Army and the evacuation of Crimea, exile was the only way out for them. Elisabeth, who was pregnant at the time, boarded the last boat at Novorossisk with her mother and her oldest daughter Gaiana (born of her first marriage) and headed for Georgia. The entire voyage was a nightmare; however, Yuri was born safe and sound at Tiflis. Lise's husband was able to join her at Constantinople where, a year later, Anastasia was born. In 1922, following the great Russian emigration, the entire family settled in Paris which had become the capital of "Russia in exile."

The Death of Her Child

In Paris the Skobtsovs had a difficult time of it due to their "persons without a country" status, which left them in a state of total poverty and insecurity. However, all of these material difficulties paled in the face of the tragic illness and death of their daughter Anastasia during the winter of 1923-24. In the end Anastasia was diagnosed with meningitis, but it was too late. The child's life ended after much suffering.

The death of Anastasia, whose name means "resurrection," broke her mother's heart. Paradoxically, through the opening caused by the agony of this loss, the living God, in whom Elisabeth had ceased to believe after her father's death, once again flooded into her life. Elisabeth experienced this new catastrophe of Anastasia's death as a mysterious divine "visitation" which was for her simultaneously the anticipation of the Last Judgment. At the dead child's side, her mother wrote these lines: "I have never known

what it meant to repent but now I see with horror how much I am repre-
hensible... throughout my entire life, I have chosen paths with no way out.
Now I want to travel on a road that is purified, filled with light. Not that I
believe in this life but to justify, understand and accept death... nothing is
greater than the commandment 'Love one another.' Go to the far reaches of
love; love without making any exception. Then all becomes clear, and life,
which otherwise would be an abominable burden, is justified."[6] Mother
Maria would later say, "The death of a loved one is the door that opens
suddenly upon eternity. In visiting us, the Lord reveals the true nature of
things: on the one hand a dead skeleton of a human being and of all creation that is mortal as he is, and on the other hand, simultaneously, the
Spirit of fire, giver of life, consoler who consumes and fills all."[7] From
then on all changed: Elisabeth's entire existence was dominated and pene-
trated by this presentiment of faith in the *eschaton*, both terrible and
joyous. "The old has passed away, the new has come," as in 2 Corinthians
5:17. The new reality is a reality of "love without limits" of which Elisabeth
felt herself called to be the living witness here and now.

> Of holiness, of good works, of dignity
> One cannot find in me. Why have you chosen me?
> I can only give up... without being able to say
> Who has knocked at my door, or when
> Calling me to struggle against all evil.
> Against death itself.
>
> O heart, know your motto. That it may shine on your standards!
> Write on your banner: "We exalt the Lord!"
> Then your hymn will sing out in the fiery flames
> Then my heart will welcome your grace.

A Diaconal Ministry

In reality, the life of Elisabeth Skobtsova would take another direction. The
relationship between Elisabeth and her husband became strained. They had
an amicable separation in 1927. Elisabeth then made a serious commitment to
the youth movement that grew up spontaneously amid the Russian emigration, the "ACER" or *Action Chrétienne d'Étudiants Russes* (the Russian Student Christian Movement). The ACER saw itself as a movement within the
Orthodox Church. Its activity was nourished by the celebration of the
eucharistic mystery. However, the movement also benefited from the

inspiration of the Russian Religious Renaissance of the beginning of the century that had reengaged in the interrupted dialogue of the nineteenth century between the intelligentsia and the Orthodox Church. Well-known intellectuals such as the Marxist economist Sergius Bulgakov and the libertarian philosopher Nikolai Berdiaev experienced a true conversion. These "great converts" whose faith had been tested in doubt became the inspiration for the young people in exile who aspired, according to their own expression, to "create an ecclesial way of life," that is to say, to penetrate life fully in all its social and personal dimensions with the light of Christ so as to render the works of culture a religion "in spirit and in truth." Ordained to the priesthood in 1918, Sergius Bulgakov taught dogmatic theology at the St Sergius Institute of Orthodox Theology, founded in 1925. He became Elisabeth's confessor and spiritual father. She had close ties as well with other brilliant members of this new Christian intelligentsia: Nikolai Berdiaev, George Fedotov (a church historian), and Konstantin Mochulskii (the biographer of Gogol and of Dostoevsky). She had a special relationship with Ilya Fundaminsky, who like Lise was a revolutionary socialist. He was of Jewish origin, but Christian in his heart.[8]

Around 1928, Elisabeth Skobtsova became the itinerant secretary of the Russian Student Christian Movement, traveling from one French university to another to visit the various Russian Christian student groups that were forming. She gave conferences all over France, in Lyons, Marseilles, Toulouse, and Strasbourg. Very quickly she understood that she could not simply limit herself to the universities. From then on she visited other groups and regions more often, from the industrialized cities of Russian immigrants working in the mines to the great tall furnaces of the newly founded chemical industry. As she journeyed, she discovered many Russians with chronic illnesses, those with tuberculosis and alcoholism, those whom no one wanted; Russians confined to psychiatric hospitals, whom no one treated because of the language barrier. She understood with much greater clarity that her vocation was not only to give brilliant lectures, but to listen, to become a confidante, to console and as much as possible to offer concrete assistance. One of her poems from this period reveals her discovery of this vocation.

> What good is clever intelligence to me
> What good are the words from books
> When everywhere I see the dead face
> Of despair, of nostalgia, of suicide.

O God, why is there no refuge?
Why so many abandoned and orphaned?
Why the wanderings of your bitter people
In this immense, eternal desert of the world!

I want only to know the joy of giving.
Oh, to console with my whole being the pains of the world.
Oh, that the fire, the cry of bloody dawns,
Might be drowned in the tears of compassion.

In reality, without actually having the title, Elisabeth was exercising the ministry of a deaconess or "spiritual mother." After her lectures, people would press forward to speak with her. Often there would be a long line leading to the room where she was seeing people, just as before a confessional. Forlorn men and women would tell her their life stories and share their most intimate crises.

And so was born within her a desire for official ecclesial recognition. Later, after becoming a monastic, she would receive from her bishop permission to preach after the divine liturgy when visiting country parishes. When she thought of asking to take vows as a monastic, she thought of the official consecration of the full offering of herself to God and to his people, to God through his people. Her desire, however, encountered many obstacles. For many of the more traditional Orthodox, Elisabeth's past political activities and particularly her two marriages were incompatible with her entry into monasticism. There is, however, a church canon of the emperor Justinian from the sixth-century "Novella," that allows divorce in cases where one of the spouses wants to enter monastic life. Daniel Skobtsov generously accepted ecclesiastical divorce from Elisabeth. With this agreement and the canon of Justinian, Metropolitan Evlogii, spiritual leader of the Russian Orthodox parishes in western Europe, now believed he could welcome Elisabeth's request. In March of 1932, in the church of the Orthodox Theological Institute of St Sergius in Paris, the ceremony of her monastic profession took place. Metropolitan Evlogii himself presided and gave the newly tonsured monastic the name of Maria, in remembrance of the great penitent saint, Mary of Egypt. Perhaps he saw in this monastic the hope for a restoration of traditional monasticism of women that was sorely lacking in his Church. Others such as Nikolai Berdiaev and Fr Lev Gillet[9] feared that the taking of the monastic habit would hold Mother Maria back from realizing her true vocation.

Monasticism Open to the World

During the summer after her monastic profession, Mother Maria visited several different women's monastic communities in the Baltic countries, Latvia and Estonia, the old provinces of the Russian Empire where there was a traditional monastic life. She returned from these travels more aware than ever that these traditional forms of monasticism were not appropriate for the situation of the Russian emigration in western Europe. She experienced these traditional forms of monasticism as being antiquated and contaminated by a bourgeois spirit, something that for her was antithetical to the true radical authentic monastic vocation. For many women, Mother Maria believed, monasticism was a means of founding a spiritual family that offered refuge, security, and "high walls of protection against the ugliness and misery of the world." This notion of monasticism, she thought, could possibly be appropriate at other times in our history. But this was an apocalyptic time, when the end of the world seemed to be at hand. One must not forget that Mother Maria's concept of monasticism was developed in the 30's when fascism, the rise of the vile beast, was at its height. But it goes much further than that. Under the influence of Fr Lev Gillet, Mother Maria rediscovered the dynamic eschatological quality of early Christianity. Mother Maria dreamt of a creatively renewed monasticism that would be a response to the vocation discerned in the "signs of the times": monasticism not lived out behind protective walls but "in the world," metaphorically speaking: fire and coals lit in the middle of the city as the great, largely unrecognized, Russian theologian Alexander Bukharev wanted.[10]

To monks and nuns, Mother Maria believed she had to make this appeal: "Open your doors to homeless thieves... let the world enter. Let them destroy your magnificent liturgical edifices. Humble yourselves... empty yourselves—humility having no comparison to that of our God. Take on the vow of poverty in all its devastating rigor. Reject all comfort, even monastic comfort. May your hearts be purified by fire so that they might leave behind all comfort. Then you will be able to say, my heart is ready, my heart is ready..."[11] For us all, we must take seriously the Gospel parable of the Last Judgment. And Mother Maria gave this exhortation: "The path toward God passes through love of our neighbor and there is no other way. At the Last Judgment, we will not be asked if we succeeded in our ascetic exercises. We will not be questioned about the number of genuflections we've made during prayer. We will be asked if we fed the hungry, clothed the naked, visited the sick and the prisoners. For each poor person, each hungry person, each prisoner, the Lord says, 'That is I. I was hungry, I was thirsty, I was sick and in prison.'"[12]

A House Open to All

The beginning of the 1930's was marked by a severe economic crisis in France. The Russian immigrants were often the first victims. Mother Maria decided to open a house where, as long as there was some space left, all those who came, no matter who they were, could receive a welcome as brothers and sisters. She had no money but, inspired by the apostle Peter, her eyes fixed on the Lord, she felt she needed to learn how to walk on water. Thanks to many gifts (often received from her Anglican friends), she was able to acquire a house in the seventh district of Paris at No. 9 Villa de Saxe. This house was too cramped. So she bought a house in disrepair on Lourmel Street in the fifteenth district. The Russian nun with the big smile, hair unkempt and habit stained with the traces of her work in the kitchen or in the studio, became a popular figure. At "Lourmel Street," the customary way of referring to this monastic dwelling, lived three monastics, one priest, a chaplain, a theology professor, some people without work or money, Russian ex-prisoners who at the end of their sentences had nowhere to go, and those who had been released from psychiatric hospitals by Mother Maria's intervention. She saw them as healthy in mind and spirit and did not count them as dangerous. At Lourmel Street, former prostitutes could also be found whom Mother Maria had taken off the streets. Sometimes there would be artists and dancers of the Russian Opera or members of the Catholic Gregorian Choir.[13] One of the chaplains referred to this as "pandemonium."

A chapel complete with painted or embroidered icons made by Mother Maria was arranged in the courtyard. She had the hands of an angel and decorated the chapel with love. Regular services and the divine liturgy were celebrated by the priest assigned to the house. For several years, this ministry was exercised by Fr Lev Gillet, a French monk who loved and encouraged Mother Maria. At times she was deeply inspired by him. In 1938, when Fr Lev left France, a young married priest, Fr Dimitri Klepinin, took over. Mother Maria, however, did not manage the long Byzantine services very well. She admitted they often bored her. She attended sporadically. She had so much to do!

She cooked and did the shopping at the market. At dawn she was already at the market where the shopkeepers knew her and would give her significant discounts or simply offer her some of the things that would not keep. Sometimes she would spend the night in a cafe near the market with the homeless who could remain there for the price of a glass of wine. She would speak with them and invite them to Lourmel Street, especially those Russians who had been abandoned by everyone, to come and see in an attempt to find solutions to their problems. Fr Lev Gillet would often go with her. In one of his talks he made reference to her gifts: her ability to listen, her tremendous compassion for sinners, her respect for the poor and humble. They were called to her. The Lord said, "Go live in the midst of the poor and homeless. Between you and them, between the world and me, create a bond that nothing can break."

Deaconess without actually having the title, Mother Maria was none the less a typical intellectual Russian. In her monastic habit, she would occasionally smoke in public, something that scandalized those who saw her. She attracted much criticism. Although she was an authentic social worker, she loved engaging in theological or philosophical discussions well into the night. "The Academy of Religious Philosophy," which was founded by Berdiaev, met at Lourmel Street. She took part in their gatherings. In 1935 she founded Orthodox Action with some friends. This was at the same time an organization administering and coordinating ever-increasing social activities,[14] and a free spiritual fellowship of Orthodox Christian inspiration and reflection. As such this organization published a journal entitled *Novyi grad* (The New City). Religious, social, and political themes were discussed in a spirit of ecumenism. In its fundamental nature, *Novyi grad* was very close to the journal *Esprit* (Spirit), founded at the same time by Emanuel Mounier. Berdiaev was also a collaborator.

During these years Mother Maria experienced yet another loss. In Russia, her eldest daughter, Gaiana, died. Following the advice of André Gide, she returned to Russia at this time. To make matters worse, in those days the atmosphere at the house on Lourmel Street was very tense. Two factions developed and created conflict. One was the group related to Orthodox Action with Mother Maria; the other rallied around Mother Eudoxia, another monastic who joined the community. Mother Eudoxia, a woman of great character, was opposed to Mother Maria in that she espoused a more traditional view of monasticism based on the *opus Dei*, the regular celebration of the cycle of liturgical services. The conflict was poisoned by the presence of a pious and knowledgeable archimandrite, Fr Kiprian Kern, who lacked all sympathy for Mother Maria. He did not understand her vision of things. Fr Kiprian supported Mother Eudoxia. Instead of facilitating peace, he only added fuel to the fire. Mother Maria suffered greatly from this lack of understanding; however, she managed to overcome any spirit of bitterness as she expressed in this poem written at about this time:

> I know it, the stake will be lit
> by the calm hand of a sister
> my brothers will go to fetch wood
> and even the most gentle
> on my sinful path
> will say cruel words.
>
> My pyre will burn
> hymns of my sisters
> peaceful sounding of the bells
> in the Kremlin on the execution square
> or else here in this foreign land
> where piety is like a weight.
>
> From the dry branches, a slender smoke trail rises
> Fire appears at my feet
> the funeral chant becomes louder
> But the shadows are not dead or empty
> In their midst the Cross
> my end burned away.[15]

The End

Mother Maria had a presentiment long before the Second World War broke out in 1939. After the collapse of 1940, there was the German occupation. The scarcity of food hit poor people the hardest. Then there was the hunting down of the Jews, beginning with foreign Jews. Mother Maria, whose best friend was the Russian Jew Ilya Fundaminsky, did not hesitate for a moment. She knew what path to take. Her home quickly became known as a refuge for Jews. There, those who were in danger were hidden before offering them clandestine passage to the free zone. Fr Dimitri Klepinin drew up false baptismal documents for those who needed them. These things were known. It is said that Mother Maria was betrayed by someone who ate at her table.

On February 8, 1943, the Gestapo came during her absence to arrest her son Yuri, who was a student, Fr Dimitri, and Fyodor Pianov, the administrator of Orthodox Action. Mother Maria was told that they all would be freed if she turned herself in to the German police. When she came down to the station, she, too, was arrested. Her son and her friends were not released. All four were deported to the concentration camps: the men to Buchenwald, Mother Maria to Ravensbruck. Only Pianov would return.

Gifted with an exceptional amount of energy, and sustained by an unquenchable faith, Mother Maria was well armed to resist the terrible testing of the concentration camp. "Everyone on our cell block knew each other," one of her cellmates remembered. "She got along with the young and the old, with people of more liberal persuasion, with believers and unbelievers... In the evening, gathered around her miserable bed, we listened to her... She spoke to us of her work in Paris, of her hope that one day we would experience unity between the Catholic and Orthodox churches. Thanks to her, we regained our strength when we were crushed by the increasing weight of terror and felt ourselves ready to give out."[16]

Secretly Mother Maria was able to obtain some embroidery thread that she had traded for a ration of bread. She continued to embroider icons and even did a symbolic fresco representing the arrival of the Normans in Great Britain. But the last months before the liberation were terrible. Afflicted with dysentery, Mother Maria grew weaker. On a piece of paper she scratched out a message to Metropolitan Evlogii and to her spiritual father, Fr Sergius. "Here is my present understanding of things: I fully accept suffering... And I want to welcome death, if it comes, as a grace from on high." She, who so many times offered comfort to others, was in silence now, as if plunged into an inner dialogue of which one of her poems speaks:

Here the soul is riveted in its essential solitude,
Only I and Thou. Thy light, my sin
Here I am, having reached my limit
Thy sun breaks forth in the East.

It is not known exactly how Mother Maria died. Separated from the cellmates of her block, she was transferred to the youth camp where the sick and disabled were left to die of malnutrition. She must have died in complete solitude and deprivation. Some believe that they saw her name on a list of prisoners who were sent to the gas chamber on March 31, 1945.[17] It is said that she took the place of a young Polish woman condemned to die in the gas chamber. A few days later in the beginning of April, the camp was disbanded in the face of advancing Russian troops.

The destiny of Mother Maria Skobtsova may seem to some like a complete waste. Her two marriages ended in divorce. Her children died prematurely. She held herself responsible for the arrest of her son. She did not see the victory over the Nazi barbarians, although she never ceased to hope in this. Orthodox Action barely survived. In the Orthodox monastic life, she had no followers. Nonetheless, she lives. Her passionate appeals do not cease to question and awaken Orthodox Christians today. Can we compare her influence in the Orthodox Church after her death to that of Dietrich Bonhoeffer in the Protestant world? Just like Bonhoeffer, she aspired to a Christianity open to the secular world. And especially above and beyond all the paralyzing structures, she calls us to go forward toward him who comes.

One of her friends told of a dream in which he saw Mother Maria walking in the midst of a field of wheat. He cried out to her: "How is this possible, Mother Maria? They told me you were dead!" Peering over her glasses and gently fixing her mischievous gaze upon him, she quipped, "People tell tales. You see quite well that I am alive!" The Monk of the Eastern Church told me this dream. He said of Mother Maria Skobtsova, "She is a modern Orthodox saint."

The Yellow Star

A Poem by Mother Maria Skobtsova, Paris, 1942

Two triangles, one star,
The crest of our ancestor David
This is a choice, not an offense
A great gift, not an ordeal

Israel, you are persecuted
once again. But what importance is hatred
of men, if in the storm on Mount Zion
Elohim responds anew.

May those who wear the seal
The seal of the hexagonal star
Know how to reply with a free soul
To the sign of servitude.

NOTES

1. For the publication of these biographical notes, I referred essentially to the work of Sergei Hackel, *One, of Great Price* (London: Darton, Longman & Todd, 1965). (Ed. note: also published in the United States under the title *Pearl of Great Price* [Crestwood, NY: St Vladimir's Seminary Press, 1981].) A collection of Mother Maria's poems appeared in Russian under the title, *Mat' Mariia* (Paris: Oreste Zeluck Editions, 1947). I have also cited some of her poems in the French translation that appeared in the journal *Contacts*, no. 51, 1965, which was devoted to her. In the same journal, no. 100, 1977, we find reminiscences of Mother Maria by C. Mochoulskii. For a significant essay of Mother Maria, "Types of Religious Lives," only recently located in her mother's archives and translated by Fr Alvian Smirensky, see *Sourozh*, nos. 74-76, 1998-99, pp. 4-10, 13-27, 21-35.

2. S. Hackel, *op. cit.,* pp. 76.

3. Among the friends of her family was the Ober-Procurator of the Holy Synod, Pobedonostsev. He was particularly taken with Elisabeth.

4. Concerning this period, see Nicolas Zernov, *The Russian Religious Renaissance of the Twentieth Century* (New York: Harper & Row, 1963).

5. Having emigrated to France, Dmitrii Kuzmin-Karavaev converted to Roman Catholicism (as did Viacheslav Ivanov) and entered the Jesuit order.

6. S. Hackel, *op. cit.,* p. 4.

7. Ibid., p. 5.

8. Fundaminsky was baptized by Fr Dimitri Klepinin at the camp of Compiegne, just before his deportation to Germany.

9. Fr Lev Gillet was the first priest of the French language Orthodox parish founded in Paris in 1929. He was a close friend of Mother Maria. He is the author of a number of spiritual writings which he signed "A Monk of the Eastern Church." He also wrote *Orthodox Spirituality,* 2nd ed. (Crestwood, NY: St Vladimir's Seminary Press, 1996) and a work called *Judaism and Christianity: Communion in the Messiah.* See the journal *Contacts,* no. 116, 1981. See also E. Behr-Sigel, *Un Moine de L'Église d'Orient* (Paris: Cerf, 1993), ch. 7. (Ed. note: now translated by Helen Wright as *Lev Gillet, a Monk of the Eastern Church* [Oxford: Fellowship of St Alban and St Sergius, 1999].)

10. In reference to Alexander Bukharev, see E. Behr-Sigel, *Alexandre Boukharev, Un Théologien de l'Église Orthodoxe Russe en dialogue avec le monde moderne* (Paris, 1973). See also Paul Evdokimov, *Le Christ dans la pensée Russe* (2nd ed., Paris: Cerf, 1986), pp. 85-89.

11. S. Hackel, *op. cit.,* p. 26.

12. Ibid., pp. 29-30.

13. I took these details from a letter addressed to me by Fr Lev Gillet when he was chaplain at Lourmel Street.

14. She founded a retirement home for the elderly and infirm at Noisy-le-Grand. [Ed. note: This house is no longer functioning today, but all of the icons in its chapel, by Fr Gregory Krug, have been placed in the newly built chapel of the Znaménié Monastery in Marcenat.]

15. *Contacts,* no. 51, 1965, pp. 223-224. Peace returned to the house at Lourmel Street when Mother Eudoxia left to found her own community, the Monastery of the Protection of the Mother of God in Bussy-en-Othe in the department of Yonne.

16. S. Hackel, *op. cit,* p. 131-132.

17. See the personal witness of Irene Vebster in *Mat' Mariia,* p. 165.

6

A Monk in the City:
Alexander Bukharev, 1822-1871[*]

In the West, the person whom Nikolai Berdiaev called "the great Russian theologian, Bukharev,"[1] is practically unknown. His prolific and varied works, written in a style that he himself characterized as coarse and muddled, have not yet been translated.[2] Lost or hidden away in archives inaccessible to the general public, today they are for all intents and purposes unable to be located in Russia.[3]

Bukharev, while he was alive, experienced social ostracism, indifference and the obscurity imposed by a totalitarian regime which attempted to erase all traces of his unique thought. His solitary way of thinking, however, cut through all of this and magnetized the great modern Russian religious thinkers. Bukharev was their forerunner. By the audacity and depth of his intuition, he blazed a trail for his many followers. The protagonists of the spiritual renaissance of the early twentieth century, including Razanov, Florensky, Berdiaev, Bulgakov, and Paul Evdokimov, the last great theologian of the Russian emigration,[4] all of whom were distinguished intellectuals, saw in Archimandrite Feodor (the monastic name and title of Bukharev) a prophetic figure, a messenger, whose message still needed to be understood. At the dawn of the Russian Revolution in the spring of 1917, a first edition of letters of the theologian to his "friends of Kazan" appeared. In the preface, Pavel Florensky wrote, "Whoever studies nineteenth century Russian cultural history will discover Bukharev as one of the most fruitful figures. His, however, was a prophetic apparition... Only the future will uncover a true understanding of Archimandrite Feodor through his unsettling works and thought, which beyond our present anticipate the future."[5]

[*] First published in *Revue d'Histoire Spirituelle*, 52, 1976, pp. 49-88. Translated by Lyn Breck.

An Incarnate Word

For the historian of Russian religious thought, the name Bukharev first evokes a destiny: that of a monk who above all else embodied in real life the prediction uttered by *Starets* Zosima to Alyosha Karamazov in Dostoevsky's novel, *The Brothers Karamazov*: "You will leave these walls... You will live in the world as a monastic." A man of prayer and contemplation, a soul of "childlike purity" witnessing to all who came near him, Archimandrite Feodor asked to be freed from his religious vows after fifteen years of exemplary monastic life. " Taking on the blame of all for all," as Fr Zosima said of the vocation of monastics, he wanted to go into the world "as a sinner under penance," an action which brought upon him the disapprobation of his friends and the plight of personal solitude, which is the fate of prophets.

Nothing allows us to affirm that these events influenced the literary works of Dostoevsky which were written later. Both of them believing Christians and contemporary thinkers, whose paths to Christianity passed through the fire of doubt, Bukharev and Dostoevsky, without knowing it, by their longings to discover a new form of Christian holiness remained true to the needs of a new spiritual era. Their intention was to unite the peaceable interior spiritual life of the monk with creativity directed toward the world of the Renaissance man, divine charity toward "the violent ones who seize the kingdom of heaven," tenderness toward this earth, compassionate solidarity toward the children of this century. Still, sketched out in the person of Alyosha, the idea of the monk in the world remains, however, in Dostoevsky's thinking, a pale attempt in the context of an uncertain doctrine.

A writer of a more liberal political persuasion yet a profound theologian, Bukharev, by contrast, situates everything in his work and his life within the vision drawn from the sources of the living Tradition of the Church. Like the Church Fathers, his mystical theology, as opposed to all purely speculative gnostic approaches, has an eminently practical sense. It illuminates a spiritual path. Being a monk in spirit while sharing the ordinary life in the world, attempting to transfigure *eros* in Christian marriage, going to the depths of hell in the secular world separated from God, discerning the light which shines in the darkness, and there showing the path to union with the compassionate God: such was the unusual vocation of Archimandrite Feodor.

Discerning in "the signs of the times" the call of the living God from whom it was impossible to hide, Bukharev accepted the risk of radical obedience to the end, even to complete disenfranchisement. Heir of the old Russian "fools for Christ sake," in the course of his life he took prophetic action. Although his decisions skirted the far edges of the law, he willingly assumed the harsh consequences. Dismissing the chance at a protected life, he hoped that in being broken himself he would break through the wall of separation. He believed that by being torn apart himself, he could forge a way through to the light of Mount Tabor, the only power capable of transforming the hideous face of this world.

Taking Root

Bukharev's spiritual roots plunged deeply into the heart of the mystical and evangelical piety of the believing Russian people. In his father, who was a humble village deacon and a simple peasant who worked the fields, he found his first theology teacher. The deacon, a man of great faith, had the gift of proclaiming his faith in strong and vivid language. One day his child asked, "God is poor, isn't he, because he takes their side and tells them to practice charity?" "God is rich," the father replied, " and he is the master of all things. He is attentive to the needs of the poor and adopts them as his children. He accepts the alms we give to the poor as though we were offering them to Him." Using a parable, he then tried to explain the mystery of redemption to his son: "God in his great love for us sinners came to earth in a visible form. He became man. He was a little child like you. He took all our misfortunes upon himself and especially all our sin. It's as though from your window you see a man in the street who is wavering under the weight of a burden that is too heavy for him. So you, who are strong, hurry to his side and take his burden upon your shoulders. This is the way in which God loves such as ourselves, the poor."[6] Bukharev himself understood that his intuition of divine compassion, the beginnings of his Christian life, came from the heart of a believing people.

Like many extraordinary thinkers, Bukharev focused on one thought in different forms, drawn from a unique experience of revelation bearing inexhaustible fruit: the revelation of God who humbles himself so that we might be exalted, who through love transcends his own transcendence, God who from all time offers the generous gift of himself, and whose glory shines forth in this ineffable giving of himself. This paternal story holds the seed of all of Bukharev's theology, his kenotic Christology. As he matured, he conscientiously increased his sense of a compassionate and victorious God, suffering with and for man, bearing the crushing weight of the world in a mysterious *kenosis*. [Ed. note: Christ's self-emptying of Phil 2:7] This would become the dynamic center of integration around which his vision of the world in God would develop. Here lay the key to the understanding of the signs of the times and of his own destiny.

Becoming a Man

At the age of fourteen, the young Bukharev entered the Church seminary of Tver (Kalinin). There, over the course of his years of study, he experienced a spiritual crisis characterized by a "painful sense of depersonalization." His heart remained faithful but his wandering, curious intelligence was attracted to the sirens of German philosophy. In particular, he was drawn to the philosophy of Hegel. At that time, a well known propagandist, Bielinsky, was devoted to spreading the word about Hegel in Russia.

Like the Pied Piper of Hamelin, Bielinsky gathered Russian students and led them to the great Hegelian river which soon became a tidal wave. Bielinsky's atheism, cloaked in noble humanitarianism, seriously impressed the young Dostoevsky. At times, Bielinsky even spoke the language of the Gospel. The young seminarian Bukharev made a mistake, but what a providential mistake it was! From this dive "into the depths of perverted thinking in regard to the truth of Christ," he emerged enriched, fortified in the faith, "blinded by the abundance of Christ-like light which is revealed to the believer." At the source of Hegel's thought, our courageous explorer discovered the temporal aspects of the Judaeo-Christian revelation, the age of the Gospel which was not a poor reflection of eternity but rather the space of God's patience and freedom for his people, the dimension where God's benevolent plan is realized: "to bring the age to its completion, to reunite the entire universe under one leader, Jesus Christ, who is in the heavens and on earth" (Eph 1:10).[7]

This work of discernment and integration continued during Bukharev's student years at the Ecclesiastical Academy of Moscow, considered the greatest place of Orthodox theological teaching during the nineteenth century. He was accepted as a student of the academy in 1842. There he spent twelve years that were particularly important for his preparation, first as a student and then as a teacher. It was here, in the monastic peace of this Lavra of St Sergius and the Trinity,[8] that he struggled with the angel. Just like Jacob, he came out of it wounded at the hip but also the winner. Obsessed by the eternal question of Job, about which Bielinsky himself painfully observed that Hegelian philosophy gave no valid response, the young man found himself prey to doubt, torn apart in the depths of his soul. "Peace returned only at the moment of supreme surrendering before the crucified yet victorious Lord on the cross," he would confide in Anna Bukhareva much later. Nevertheless, converted to the God of Abraham, Isaac, and Jacob, the God of Jesus Christ, Alexander as a student recognized in this God, the one whose muffled cries had already reached him through "the ideas of the philosophers."

Having come to the end of his studies, Alexander announced his intention to enter monastic life. The decision astonished his friends and family, for it appeared to be in complete contradiction with his passionate interest in secular culture. In reality, a judgment of God to which he submitted himself through his father-confessor's intervention put an end to this agonizing period of indecision.[9] Welcomed in a spirit of faith and obedience, the divine word first overwhelmed him and then delivered him from the weight, such that "even the weakness from which he suffered left him at that time."

Several months after this event, Alexander was tonsured a monk. At his monastic profession, which was immediately followed by his ordination to priesthood, he was given the name Feodor. He was kept on at the seminary, and as a young hieromonk (priest-monk) he was given the rank of professor of theology. As such, he taught hermeneutics of both the Old Testament and the New, an approach that was particularly difficult given that the methods of historical criticism and scientific exegesis had only just recently begun to find acceptance in the Orthodox theological schools.

These first years of monastic life were characterized by intense intellectual work and spiritual fervor. Having first had misgivings that monasticism would distance him from the world and earthly existence, enclosing him in a solitary quest for transcendent salvation, he soon experienced his new life as an "angelic" spiritual ministry in the communion of love without limits. "Monastic life is called angelic," he affirmed,

> because monks, like angels, are called to serve all and to work for the salvation of mankind. Their vocation in its essence does not differ from that of other Christians, in particular that of married couples. But the monastic

vocation surpasses that of marriage in its emphasis on the universal. Married couples must discern, cherish, and respect the image of God in each other. The monk, in taking the monastic vow of celibacy, prepares himself to 'see through the vision of faith the Lord himself in each person.' In all his relationships, he desires only to gain Christ. Strangers as well as family and friends, honest and dishonest people alike, all are for the untarnished soul the true bridegroom, Jesus Christ. Inspired by the love of Christ...the man of God opens his arms to each one.[10]

While praying in church, the young monk was overcome by a presentiment of a "spiritual springtime." Everything had become new. The holy figures of the apostles and saints on the iconostasis were inhabited by a mysterious life. They were "the living ones" who saw and blessed him. Simultaneously his heart became "vulnerable." When reading the verse in the Psalms, "Truth will come forth from the earth and justice will pervade the heavens," (Ps 84/85:12) his soul was filled with an infinite gentleness.

> From Feodor's perspective, the Church became a vast expanse, so vast as to fill the dimensions of the universe. His prayer rose toward the mystery of the Trinity whose radiant glory enlightens the cosmos and enlivens the history of mankind. Enacting the divine compassion for the destiny of the world, the Son leads humanity, under the protection of the Holy Spirit, toward the kingdom of heavenly grace.[11]

Bukharev never denied this luminous vision of humanity moving toward its fulfillment in God. However, a more sober understanding stripped away his romantic tendencies. In its center and as its sun, the cross of the victorious slain Lamb who bears the sins of the world would rise up. "Do you know what thought now comes to mind?" he wrote in 1863, the day after a distressing experience.

> It's the idea of God filling the entire universe, in all its earthly and human reality, and of all that is earthly and human rising up to God: each one according to the grace of God made man who, having taken upon himself the burden of all evil, pours out the fullness of his blessings upon humanity. This is my theology, this is my philosophical vision of the world! I exult for joy... Evil and lies may be cunning and tempestuous. But taken up and away on the shoulders of him who is truth and sovereign good, they are dismantled and shattered in their basic essence and in their effects. Christ, the life and truth of life, by his death trampled down him who holds the power of death, the devil. (cf. Heb 2:14)[12]

A profound optimism as well as a sorrowful joy threads its way through all of Bukharev's works and life. Their foundation is faith, faith in the triumphant God, in the "compassionate God, the Lover of mankind," according to the beautiful expression of the Byzantine liturgy. At the heart of this theologian's meditation is the mystery of Christ, both God and man, of the humbling of the Son to the point of death on the cross, "to the realization of the unimaginable abandonment by the Father," the mystery of compassion and sacrificial love which could be none other than Christ, both God and man. "God became man so that man could become god," according to the patristic saying.

For Bukharev, it was less a question of speculation on the ontological aspects of this mystery than it was to seize Christ's "virtue" and his "spirit," the spirit of love by which Christ's death conquered death. The goal of Christian existence is to "gain Christ," that is, to receive the Holy Spirit who binds us to himself. This is the traditional teaching of the Orthodox Church. At times, however, a pseudo-spiritualism distorts this true meaning of the Christian life, holding in disdain the human, earthly aspects and advocating a detachment from historic responsibilities. Nothing in this traditional Orthodox view of things supports such escapism. The Spirit is given to the Christian so that he might participate in Christ, by having communion in his sacrificial love, for the salvation and transfiguration of the world here and now.

As Bukharev wrote,

The spirituality of our life and our actions is not a flight that distances us from our human condition, from the concrete reality of our bonds with family, country, or city. These realities have been assumed by the Son of God himself, and have been united to God in the fullness of his person, of his soul, thoughts, feelings, human will, and desires. The gift of the Holy Spirit, which frees us from the vanities of this rotting and fallen world, are manifested by the fulfillment in Christ of all things. This manifestation is revealed from bodily functions to higher thought processes, by seeking in Christ, in communion with the Spirit of the Father. This is the source of solutions to both temporal and ecclesiastical problems.[13]

Contrary to the Hegelian historical pantheism, world history for Bukharev is not a holy history. Rather a holy history is fulfilled in the world: that of the Church of the Holy Spirit, the martyrs, prophets, and all witnesses of the faith both known and unknown who have given their lives to hasten the coming of the kingdom, the reconciliation in Christ of all things, "both heavenly and earthly."

Orthodoxy and the Contemporary World

Until 1860, Feodor's academic and ecclesiastical career unfolded quite normally. He was elevated to the rank of archimandrite as a young man. However, he had several painful encounters with his superiors, especially the well-known Metropolitan Philaret of Moscow, who held the young professor in great affection and admiration and was attentive to his career. The Metropolitan, however, was concerned about Feodor's interest in the problems of contemporary city life, thinking this preoccupation to be unseemly for a man of the Church and particularly for a monk.

In 1854, Archimandrite Feodor was transferred from the Academy of Moscow to the one in Kazan where he became the dean of students and teacher of dogmatic theology and missions. Ascetically lean, small, and somewhat stunted, "but gifted with warm, inspired speech," Fr Feodor had a definite influence on the seminarians. Many became his disciples, then his friends. They remained faithful to him until his death and beyond. His influence extended far beyond the Academy and attracted cultured lay people. A circle of friends gathered around him. Students and bureaucrats, teachers and women of the world, noble landed gentry and progressive liberals, all mixed together. Feodor called it "our monastery," a monastery in the world where he found greater understanding and sympathy than in the halls of the official academy. However, at that time he also became the butt of jokes proffered by the rector who was jealous of his authority and often treated him as an "illuminated soul" or a "fool for Christ."

Feodor considered retreating to an isolated smaller monastic house, a skete. But in 1858 he was named as a member of the Committee of the Ecclesiastical Court in St Petersburg. This decision sealed his fate. His new responsibilities put him in contact with writers, editors, and directors of journals. Deprived of his student audience, he wrote articles that were published in various ecclesiastical or other Christian journals. In 1860, two of his books were published, one after the other. The first was *Three Letters to Gogol*, a work which laid dormant for a long time on a shelf, and the other was a collection entitled *Orthodoxy and the Contemporary World*, the only one of Bukharev's works that reached a wider public.

In order to understand the repercussions of this work, it is necessary to situate them in their context, namely the crisis of society and Russian culture in the mid-nineteenth century, which was in essence a spiritual crisis that was a prelude to the bloody encounters of the following century.

The years that Fr Feodor spent at St Petersburg were crucial for Russia. They coincided with a critical moment in his own history, the consequences of which reverberate to this day. It was a time of great hopes when Alexander II inaugurated tremendous social reforms, including the abolition of serfdom and sweeping legal reforms. A peaceful evolution from an autocracy to a more liberal, socially minded monarchy inspired by evangelical principles seemed to make the changes accessible to all people of good will. Could it be now that the reconciliation of two great Russian spiritual traditions would occur, the Christian tradition of old Russia, whose darkened paths were illumined by the light of Christ, the divine Logos, together with the Russia of the Enlightenment, born in the eighteenth century and attracted to, even fascinated by western rational thought? Would it not be the vocation of Russian culture to unite the fervor of faith to the rigor of thought, contemplation to historical effectiveness? This dream, which had already been sketched out by the philosopher Kireevskii, haunted Archimandrite Bukharev in his endless wanderings through the "city of Peter," the city that served as an immense and marvelous bridge between eastern and western Christians, built at the cost of many tears and much blood. Tragically, these years which might have sealed a reconciliation in the society instead created a definitive split in cultivated Russian society "into two antagonist camps between which," as Bukharev wrote in his *Three Letters to Gogol,* "war raged."

By the first half of the nineteenth century, Slavophiles and Westernizers brandished their opposing ideologies. These adversaries nevertheless shared a common language. Intellectuals such as Khomiakov, Kireevskii, and Herzen, while opposed to each other, were brought together on account of their mutual respect. Around 1850, under the influence of the modern liberal leftist thought of Hegel and Feuerbach, a radical split occurred. With the rise of Bielinsky, Nikolai Chernyshevsky and others who would soon be known as the nihilists, a generation of deadly "sons" and "fathers" set themselves up as a kind of religious order of atheists, soon to become the Russian pre-revolutionary intelligentsia. This group was generally devoted to serving the very people who did not embrace their vision. Having become prisoner to a blind and destructive fanaticism, the newly formed nihilists left the Church in anger and disdain, feeling betrayed by its collusion with the hateful regime. It had been their Church, the source of their ideals of sacrificial humility, even though they espoused these ideals in a distorted fashion.[14]

As a witness to this "schism," Archimandrite Feodor in his prophetic lucidity was aware of the serious potential consequences. Just like the split caused by the "Old Believers" in the seventeenth century, the new division deprived the Church of its vital force and life-blood. Bukharev sensed that the apparently humanistic hopes of these intellectual atheists, cut off from their spiritual roots and grafted onto a crude materialism, would end up at nihilism, destroying all likeness in man to the image of God and leading to a dehumanization of the culture. Going beyond the political and cultural aspects of this crisis, Feodor perceived the true spiritual meaning. It was not only the czarist state and the Church as social institutions that were in danger. It was also the humanity of man that was threatened with a "catastrophe" in the true sense of the word. Meditating on the Apocalypse of the evangelist John, on which he was writing a commentary, Bukharev saw in this crisis the moment that precedes divine judgment on a period in history. So the "What is to be done?,"[15] characteristic of the generations of the 1860's turned up repeatedly in Archimandrite Feodor's writings.

Feodor, as a monk of the Monastery of Holy Trinity-St Sergius, where he took his vows, considered himself to be a spiritual son of the founder of the Northern Thebaid. At the period in history when the Tartar maurauders roamed freely, St Sergius of Radonezh had pleaded with the rival Russian princes to maintain the peace. Much like St Sergius,[16] Feodor felt he had a mission of reconciliation "just when a catastrophe was threatening Russia, the Church, and the world." Archimandrite Feodor's book was the ultimate attempt to reconcile the princes of contemporary thought in the radiance of Christ, the God-man. His hope was to reach the agitators of this fatal schism, the instigators of the "new humanity" in the crystal palace of the secular city. But he also engaged the men of the Church, recognized defenders of the faith, who were equally responsible for the disaster. He called them to convert to the true spirit of Orthodoxy, leaving behind their rigid, inhuman, "letter of the law" approaches to Christianity in order to adopt the Spirit of God, *philanthropos*, the "Lover of mankind." Instead of putting the light of the Gospel under the bushel of dead ritualism, one had to place it on a lampstand to illumine the whole house. Restoring to the Gospel its entire power and living force, it was necessary to clear up the error in which the Gospel was foundering or at least seemed to be. The principal error consists in basing the greatness of God upon the contempt of man's creativity, to wrongly compare as incompatible the long and patient construction of a more just and humane earthly city to the anticipation of the heavenly kingdom.

As can be seen in all of Bukharev's works, he consistently proclaimed that the God of Jesus Christ is not the "bewitching absolute where humanity is diluted like a drop of water in a vast ocean... Christ, God by his own self, assures the integrity of our personal existence."[17] And again, "He who holds the universe by the power of his word" (Heb 1:3) created "man in his own image," which means "in the image of him who is the accessible image of the inaccessible Father." He is bound to his creation by an eternal pact of love that even sin cannot destroy. "For what does all the sin of the world mean compared to the total self-giving of him by whom the world exists?"[18]

In Jesus Christ, uniting in his person "human nature by which he is of our race, to his impassable divinity... the Lamb of God slain from the beginning... takes upon himself all the sin of the world, even to death on the cross, even to the unfathomable abandonment of the Father." This is the fullness of man. Iin "the integrity of his full personhood [he] is taken into God, forgiven, sanctified and deified in hope. Such is Orthodox doctrine which the theologian affirms, contrary to the Arian and Mono-thelite heresies that 'erode the foundations of faith offered to the believer.'[19] In the God-man, all virtue, all justice, love, holiness, beauty, all divine fullness are accessible to us from now on if only we freely follow him in faith, if only we fight the good fight in order to win these treasures." Because it affirms that man's future is in God, in the God-man who is also the crucified conqueror, Christian faith is enriched with an invincible dynamism. It carries an insatiable urgency for the transformation of the world, for the transfiguration of humanity by the energies of the Holy Spirit. Such is the mystery whose revelation may hasten the return of modern schismatics to the Church.

Bukharev, in his *Concerning Orthodoxy*, challenges the claim that humanistic atheism is the right belief. Aligning himself with patristic anthropology, he denies the existence of a given human nature, "existing in and of itself, possessing that... which belongs only to God." A human being is a created freedom moving between the depths of grace and a potentiality that is only realized in the fullness of the God-man. If man is unfaithful to his vocation as a son of God according to grace and attempts to become sufficient unto himself, "he falls from divine heights to the level of a simple animal and even lower." Using the symbolic apocalyptic language of Jewish and Christian traditions, to which he devoted several studies, Bukharev envisioned the ascent of a terrifying bestial humanity.[20] While taking on the appearances of intelligence, refined culture, and even philanthropy, deformed humanity conceals, "under the appearance of a human face," powers that are destructive of the face of authentic humanity. Christian spiritual warfare is not of flesh and blood. Rather it is the warfare of the last days when the humanity of man is at stake. In the face of such a mounting threat, the Christian warrior might be gripped by fear unless he holds firmly to the foundation of his faith and hope: "Life and the word of life, Christ himself, by his death will destroy him who holds the power of death."[21] While awaiting the final victory of which we catch a glimpse in hope, it behooves each believer, each knight of the faith, to fight against the adversary who sows disorder in our hearts not only outside the Church but even in front of the sanctuary.

Bukharev then asks whether the gross materialism of "the new pagans," the prideful revolt of atheistic humanism, will in fact be the blind response to an inhuman and rigid Christianity? Orthodoxy that is rigidly faithful to the letter of the law yet "merciless to man and estranged from the spirit of the love of Christ" engenders a disastrous heresy of thought based on an equally disastrous spiritual practice. *Concerning Orthodoxy* opposes a "pseudo-spiritualism" which makes of Christianity a sentimental religion that isolates people in their social context from the spiritual realism of the Gospel and teachings of the Fathers of the Church. As a "member of a family and citizen of a state, Christ took on our humanity in all its political and social dimensions as well." If these areas are no longer under his lordship, if spiritual life is reduced to an enclosed garden of private piety, then we will "fall into an Arianism or a practical semi-Arianism" that denies the full divinity of the Son, his divine sovereignty that Christians need to confess not only with their lips but also in their actions.[22]

Archimandrite Feodor's message cannot be reduced, however, to the preaching of a social Christianity applied to an abstract Orthodoxy. It is a call to the rediscovery of the true man hidden in the heart, *homo cordis absconditus*, evoking the descent of the Spirit into the depths. Of significance is the fact that Bukharev's work begins with a quote from Metropolitan Philaret commenting on the parable of the treasure hidden in the field. "The treasure is the kingdom of heaven…hidden in the depths of man's interior." We are called to take possession of that which we already possess, to become open to the light which already shines in the deepest part of ourselves. But from this inner sanctuary of the heart, illumined by the light of Christ, a light will shine upon the entire world "so that the world will be renewed and saved."[23] The new creation begins in the hearts of men and only those who are truly spiritual can change the face of the world. It is to this task and this spiritual warfare that God calls us today.

In spite of the heaviness of his clumsy syntax, Bukharev's work impressed his readers with its freshness. Its newness was both a source of renewal and revolution. Nourished by the writings of the Fathers who were rediscovered by his generation, Archimandrite Feodor was inspired by what Vladimir Lossky called "the mystical theology of the Eastern Church," a theology enlivened by spiritual experience devoted not to intellectual speculation but to the contemplation of mystical union. Bukharev was far from being a modernist. He wanted to teach none other than the *una sancta*, a synthesis of the great proclamations of the ecumenical councils. In its historical context, the only thing revolutionary about Bukharev's approach was the integral connection between this "mystical theology" and the concern for a compassionate, actively creative and transforming presence in the world. This monk was not calling for activism. Rather, he supported actions well grounded in the spirit of Christian contemplation. For him, this vocation responded to the contemporary distress of humanity.

In order to convert the world of free license and scientific positivism to Christ, it is necessary for the fullness of the God-man to become visible in the earthly reality. It is this reality that modern man had made into an alienating idol, but which, through the lens of faith, of hope, and of love, is also the receptacle of God's divine glory. The authentic witness of this vision of a world fashioned and sustained by God is possible only by attitudes and actions. This vision then becomes an inspiration to participate in the formation of human culture. In full identification with the kenotic activity of the Son of God, those who are truly spiritual must descend to the plain, where the sick and those held captive by demons moan, far from their desire to establish their tents on Mount Tabor. They must share the passion of crucified love. Bukharev's boldness was to avoid generalities and abstractions. Inviting Christians to existentially take upon themselves the mystery of the incarnation, he asked them to engage in contemporary warfare in order to assure human freedom and dignity. He called the Church to take on the cause of the emancipation of serfs, to denounce hostilities perpetrated in the name of Christ whose "blood does not cry vengeance but implores mercy," to oppose all oppression of spirit and body!

While *Concerning Orthodoxy* was favorably received in both the liberal milieu and by a handful of young theologians close to the Academies of Moscow and St Petersburg, it was ferociously attacked by the editor of the weekly *Domashniaia Beseda*, V. I. Askochenskii. Supposedly a purist, Askochenskii presented himself as the defender of Orthodoxy and the "sublime spirituality of Mount Athos against the pernicious influences of the modern world" which he accused Feodor of practicing outright. His true motivations seemed to be more personal.[24] Askochenskii publicly painted Bukharev as the "new Luther" and the "traitor of Orthodoxy." Repudiated by his superiors and even by Metropolitan Philaret (who had no doubt regarding Feodor's Orthodoxy but who feared a scandal), Bukharev felt pressured to resign from his post in the ecclesiastical court. He was exiled in a monastery at Pereslavl out in the country. It was here in the spring of 1862 that he learned of the confiscation of his manuscript by order of the Holy Synod. This manuscript, *Commentary on the Apocalypse*, was his lifelong work.[25] The censure authorized the confiscation of the manuscript that was already in the process of publication. It was taken from the publisher and filed in the state archives.

The arbitrary injustice of this action, "the indifference to the word of God" that it seemed to portray, wounded Father Feodor far more deeply than the prejudicial attitudes caused by this decision or the actual confiscation of his work. It was the shock that caused him to leave monasticism. In June of 1862, he made his official request to the Holy Synod to be freed from his monastic vows and returned to lay status. Simultaneously he affirmed his faithfulness to the Church and his acceptance of the churchly canons. He wanted to be a full member of the Church, but "according to the freedom of the sons of God." In his eyes, monastic obedience had value only if it was taken on in a conscious manner through personal decision. "Unable to remain any longer in what had become a false and hypocritical situation imposed by monasticism," he left, "in order to preserve within himself peace and spiritual integrity which are the true principles of the monastic life."[26]

Because of civil legislative customs which accentuated the rigidity of church rules, Bukharev's request to be laicized took him to the edge of the unknown. Defrocking was a rare occurrence then. When it happened, it publicly implicated the person being defrocked as the object of punishment associated with a sin. It had extensive implications both socially and in regard to civil law.[27] Although Bukharev was aware of this, he did not let it influence his decision. He had no hesitations about fanning the flames of the scandal by announcing his intention to marry "a young woman who shared his faith and was ready to stick by him in the struggle." He believed it was important to take on this scandal in communion with "the scandal of the cross of Christ."[28] His challenging actions were marked by evangelical integrity characteristic of the "fools for Christ's sake" in ancient Russia. Archimandrite Feodor's decision, however, was inscribed within the dialectic of the kenotic way. Its true meaning unfolded in the signs of the times.

In Bukharev's work, *On the Subject of Orthodoxy,* which offered a summary of church history, he emphasized the creativity of the Holy Spirit who manifests himself in the context of the Church. According to "the needs and particularities of each age," the Spirit brings forth new forms of witness. The blood of the first Christian martyrs was followed at the time of the ecumenical councils by the martyrdom of the doctors of the Church and the great monks. Now the crucifixion was directed toward their intellects. "Who are the new confessors of faith needed by the Church in this contemporary crisis?" he asked, after meditating on the juncture between history and grace. He formulated the answer using symbolism from Scripture: as a bride of the Song of Songs, the disciple of Christ in the modern world goes to encounter the bridegroom "in the streets and city squares." But "the Lord does not turn away from the love of the one who searches." The doubting generations, like Thomas, do not want to believe unless they can put their fingers in the nail holes. Then they will recognize that the presence of the Lord abides in those wounded by his love.

Explaining his own case using the examples of some of the desert fathers, Feodor came to this seemingly paradoxical conclusion: by officially renouncing his monastic vows, he would not only remain in the Church, but also live in the world "in spirit and in truth." Faithful to the essence of his monastic vows, to the ideal of total consecration and spiritual integrity, he believed that as a free man (free because of his vows) and yet still somehow as a monk, he was called to forge a new spiritual path. He would embrace a rigorous Christian path lived out in the world by monastic souls which would at the same time be united to Christ, filled with peace, and remain in profound solidarity with the workers of this century. Finally, by virtue of this spiritual pilgrimage, a transfiguring light would be shed on the world which in and of itself was not profane but often fell into secularism because of Christian cowardice.[29]

In letters to his close friends and spiritual children, Feodor attempted to explain this paradox. "My greatest hopes for the future of the Church and the world are founded on the unfolding grace and truth of Christ for salvation in this visible earthly reality. Insofar as this concerns you (I'm thinking particularly of all who are monastics)... a certain earthly positivism keeps the light of Christ hidden. Some may consider this vision of things pure fantasy. The essence of monastic obedience, poverty, and chastity, however, are integral to this vision. With God's help, can I not discover all that is the Lord's within this earthly reality?...I chose the monastic way so that with all my heart I could belong to the one Lord (the vow of chastity), to submit entirely to his will (the vow of obedience), and to possess nothing other than him (the vow of poverty). Even now in this new way I have chosen, I am concerned with only one thing: to be exclusively committed to the Lord's ways and to please him alone. Understand he who will."[30]

Bukharev never said that he thought the monastic tradition to be outdated. He refrained from applying his personal choices to others. Nevertheless, he believed that the same Spirit who directed the first monks to the Egyptian and Palestinian deserts was now calling other monks to a different type of monasticism. This new monastic expression requires monks to plunge into the depths of the inhuman city where God seemed absent, where the devil himself now appeared to reside. Their vocation was to become embedded in earthly humanity, not to lose their souls but, like the grain of wheat that dies to give new life, to enrich humanity with the divine energy of the God-man. Only by this sober approach full of faith, hope and love is it possible to discern the light shining in the darkness.

Only in this way can humanity be delivered from its imprisonment to experience that seed of grace present in the heart of each person and his intellectual searching. Such is the true contemporary meaning and vocation of the risen Christ's mysterious descent into hell. On these things Archimandrite Feodor meditated extensively.[31]

With singular boldness, Bukharev discussed sexuality. He identified the emotional and physiological aspects of love shared by a man and woman as the privileged place of divine revelation, even though it was often absent, obscured by egotistical passions, or buried in daily monotony. The true vocation of Christian couples welcomes the light of the Word of God into the obscure places of passion in order to ground their human union in Christ. This means that the two become one in the image of Christ's union with the Church, a difficult and yet exalted calling. The discipline of monastic spirituality within the marriage vocation can help it in achieving these goals. As he explored the marriage vocation, Bukharev discovered within it a chastity that, although different from monastic chastity, was of the same essence.

Kenosis

The last act of this play took place before the church court of Vladimir, charged with executing the judgment of the Holy Synod. The court, faced with Feodor's reputed "inflexibility," attempted to avoid a scandal first by using delay tactics. At last they accepted his request with surprising promptness, which might be explained by the Czar's personal intercession requested by Bukharev himself.[32]

On July 31, 1863, one year after his original request, Archimandrite Feodor once again became "Alexander Matveievitch Bukharev, son of a deacon of the province of Tver." He signed the document that freed him from his monastic vows and deposed him from the ranks of the clergy. In his nervousness at the moment, he tipped over the ink bottle. The ink stained his hands, an unintentional act that "in his semi-conscious state" had another significance: "Here is the image of what I am trying to do. In the eyes of men, I dirty my hands which up until now have remained without stain. May this be a lesson to me! May I always follow him whom the heavenly Father has ordained as the expiation for our sin even though he himself was sinless. May we become God's justice in Christ." Among those present in the church court that day, an old priest asked him if he

had any regrets. He could only respond to this question "from a perspective less inspired by clear thought than by instinctive feeling." He did not
regret anything, he said, because essentially he had lost nothing. "As I
commit myself to this new way, I go forward supported by the power of
the lamb who gave himself to me in the words of the bishop, 'Hold onto
this pledge for which you will one day be accountable before the throne of
God at the Last Judgment.'"[33]

And so preparing to go into the world "as a sinner without penance,"
Bukharev felt as though he was borne in the depths of his being by the
"power of the lamb." He lived out his own *kenosis* in communion with the
humility of the Son of God. This kenotic asceticism was destined to overthrow the wall of separation that prevented modern humanity from
encountering Christ. The humility was a sacrificial offering of love. Five
years earlier Archimandrite Feodor had written these prophetic lines: "We
follow the example of our Lord as he appeared before the unjust tribunal.
He stood before them as one condemned, unjustly judged, covered with
shame; but before the Father in heaven, he also took on their sins. Enter also
into the ways of the lamb of God. What other path could be more noble,
what grace more precious either on earth or in heaven?"[34] As Paul
Evdokimov accurately wrote, "Bukharev seemed like a man who had been
changed once and for all by the offering of the lamb."[35] His entire life was a
consequence of the holy upheaval.

A few days after Feodor's church court hearing, the marriage of Alexander Bukharev and Anna Rodychevskaya was blessed in the Pereslavl
church. Bukharev expected a great deal from the sacrament of marriage.
The circumstances of this "crowning," however, more resembled public
ridicule.[36] On the narrow path of humility, though, he eventually reached
a new life filled with joy. In the world and in his marriage, wrote Paul
Znamensky (friend, disciple, and first biographer of Bukharev), "Alexander Matveievitch remained the man he always had been: a monk in spirit,
a man of contemplation and faith, a man who was not of this world yet
with his feet firmly planted on the ground where our Lord walked."[37]

As one might expect and as he himself predicted, life for the man in the
world but not of the world was difficult. He dared to defy taboos. Wandering, poverty, and illness were the fate of the couple. Since he was not
allowed to live in the big cities where his intellectual life had flourished,
Bukharev moved from place to place, often staying with friends in the

Church. He continued to write. From then on, however, the journals refused his articles. His books, crafted in heavy and difficult language, were often suspect in the eyes of church authorities. Frequently published at his own expense, the books reached a limited audience. Attempts to settle outside of Russia failed, one after another. When Sachenka, his only child, died at a young age, the already vulnerable Alexander was destroyed.

In shared human love and an unalterable faith, his painful end was illumined. Those who knew him during the last years of his life, such as the historian M. P. Pogodin, said that warmth and light shone forth from the broken man. His body wasted by tuberculosis, Bukharev died on April 2, 1871, Holy Thursday, in great agony. He was buried in Pereslavl. Huge crowds mourned his passing. Among them, according to his wife Anna, were many simple people. They accompanied his casket to its final resting place. On this solemn occasion, Askochenskii once more took advantage of his position to criticize Bukharev. The church press was singularly silent. Znamensky wrote about them, "They will bury him; they will forget him."

At first glance, the dramatic destiny of Archimandrite Feodor seemed to show a historic failure. While he was alive, he remained a misunderstood prophet in spite of the admiration of a few followers. His exhortations did not reach the Church, now settled into a comfortable status quo. His attempt to renew the intelligentsia by returning to the source of living water was unsuccessful. Although inspired by a vision of the lamb of God who takes away the sins of the world, his personal *kenosis* did not rend the veil of the temple. Rather his response was one of "folly and scandal for the wisdom of the world," wrote Evdokimov, "as well as for the wisdom of a theology that was hostile to the world."[38] Bukharev was reproached for his utopian views. This fool for Christ's sake, this lost soldier of Orthodoxy was nevertheless an explorer of a spiritual path, both old and new. His discoveries bear fruit right to this day. Once we remove the historical constraints, Bukharev's effective message is a contemporary one. It is compatible with what many Christians long for: a spirituality in which the interior life, far from being a factor of exclusion, actually produces an active, prophetic Christian presence in the world and throughout history.

From the beginning of the twentieth century, Bukharev's influence, thought and personality became palpable within the sphere of Russian Orthodoxy. Some authors quote him exclusively. However, at the same time, he often exercises an anonymous influence which for obvious reasons cannot be measured. His entire theological opus is worthy of extended study. This has not yet been accomplished; however, an initial attempt has been made.[39] His spiritual legacy, which is ultimately inseparable from his theological works, is actually of greatest interest here. In conclusion I will attempt to outline a few traces of his spirituality in contemporary Orthodoxy.

Archimandrite Feodore's solitary path leads us first to the spiritual quests evident in the context of the "Russian Religious Renaissance" at the beginning of the twentieth century. His message was faithfully preserved by a few followers. It was transmitted by them, especially by Razanov, to the supporters of a "new religious conscience." The puzzling figure of a monk in the world was fascinating to them, though those who actually understood the depth of his thought were few in number. The new "seekers of God" were characterized by their syncretistic religiosity or eroticism mixed with gnosticism or aestheticism, which distanced them from Bukharev's faithfulness to the Gospel. He encouraged them, however, in their hope for a dialogue with Church officials. Nikolai Berdiaev and Pavel Florensky were among the avant-garde thinkers of the time. They discerned in Bukharev something that was of concern to them that only future generations would fully understand. Florensky, a theologian, confessor of Christ in an atheistic society, and long-term correspondent with Bukharev, died in a Stalinist concentration camp. In Florensky's life, more than his works, he is a disciple of Bukharev.

In the heart of the first Russian emigration, Bukharev's questions were taken up once again by Berdiaev, this time from a theoretical and historical perspective as well as in their practical application to movements such as Orthodox Action, in which traditional Russian piety was joined with Christian social action.[40] Between the two wars, a former revolutionary socialist who had become an Orthodox nun attempted to found a monastic life outside the cloister. This was Mother Maria Skobtsova, a woman who was open to all the problems of modern culture and all the manifestations of human distress. Her monastery of sorts was located in the heart of the city. In the fifteenth district of Paris, her house opened its doors to the unemployed, prostitutes, and former mental patients whom she had had discharged from the psychiatric hospitals. With the help of Berdiaev, the French Orthodox, and other Russian Jewish and Christian intellectuals, Mother Maria organized reflection groups and conferences of very high quality.[41] Although Mother Maria was criticized by those who were more traditional, Metropolitan Evlogii, the spiritual leader of the Russian emigration in western Europe, encouraged her. In her writings, both prose and poetry, Mother Maria never makes direct reference to Bukharev; however, his life and work were widely known at that time. In her fiery compassion for mankind, her evangelical rigor, her desire for a monasticism free from rigid enslavement, we see the same kenotic vision that inspired Archimandrite Feodor. Converted to Christ from her revolutionary socialism, she avoided using the faith as a place of fearful refuge. Rather, in her faith she found the strength that allowed her to fight the good fight against all kinds of misery and degradation of the dignity of the sons of God. For her, the monastery was not a place where one withdrew from life. According to Bukharev's understanding of the Church's vocation, it needs to be a "fire lit in the center of the city" where those who are freezing can find warmth and assistance. During the German occupation of World War II, Mother Maria welcomed Jews and those involved in the resistance movement. Deported to Ravensbruck, she died there in the gas chambers on Holy Saturday in 1945.[42]

This same prophetic inspiration can be found in the life and works of the theologian Paul Evdokimov (1901-1970). A worshipper in spirit and in truth, he never ceased, like Bukharev, to struggle against the letter of the law that kills.[43] Open to monastic culture, he saw the connection between psychoanalysis and ascetic monastic tradition. He was influenced by Bukharev's thought as he formed his own personal viewpoints. Evdokimov integrated these concepts in his personal commitment as a married lay theologian and in his later works, *Marriage: The Sacrament of Love*[44] and *Ages of the Spiritual Life*[45] in which he developed the idea of interior monasticism. By his insistence on the royal priesthood of the laity effectively engaged in the work of human culture, Paul Evdokimov directly aligned himself as a spiritual descendant of Archimandrite Feodor. Evdokimov also emphasized "the transfiguration of eros" and the meaning of conjugal love as an icon of the mutual love between Christ and his Church. Both Evdokimov and Bukharev represent an evangelical, mystical, and prophetic current which continues to quicken Orthodoxy despite the heavy trappings of Byzantine splendor.[46]

In Bukharev and his followers, one can recognize an attempt to use profound Orthodox spirituality to break through the secularism of the modern world. This vocation is identified as a new from of martyrdom. The ancient wisdom reveals new horizons. The new Christian witness is not, however, limited to the horizontal plane. Founded in the traditions of the Gospel and Eastern monasticism, the new way is inspired by a "celestial vision," the same one that struck Paul on the road to Damascus. From his youngest years, Bukharev's convictions were grounded in "God, the Lover of mankind," who carries the burden of the world. It is the vision of the crucified conqueror.

Bukharev's free-flowing theological reflection rooted in the tradition of the Church along with his personal spiritual experience allowed his early intuition to deepen. "God is love," Archimandrite Feodor proclaimed with the apostle John. His love is a love of generosity or mercy that never ceases to flow out on creation to sustain it, restore it to its original beauty since its fall. This love is also a crucified love offered from the beginning and victorious in its self-giving. This is a love which is entirely concentrated on and revealed in Christ Jesus whose name, wrote Bukharev's first biographer, "never left his lips." The Lord upon whose face Bukharev gazed looked like the Christ in the Rublev icons. It was the object of contemplation for the young monk, a divine and human face filled with both gentleness and an infinite majesty, radiating a love stronger than death. It is in the radiance of this face that Bukharev invited an encounter with each man and woman across time, from ancient history to our contemporary world. He characterized modern man as enclosed in his own hell, in a universe of things which have become opaque to the divine light shining in the darkness that the darkness cannot overcome. Modern man is walled off in his own autistic ways, incapable of a sincere dialogue with the other.

Today, to become one with Christ means descending into this hell armed only with the weapon of faith, hope, and compassionate love, Bukharev affirmed. Neither crusades against the modern world nor flight nor prostration before it will change its course, but simply interior illumination enlightened by the light that lights all men coming into the world. This is the task of people of action and reflection who likewise engage in contemplation. He refers to spiritual beings who are married couples, engaged in professions, workers in the city who work with the supreme worker, servants of communion with him who wanted to be among us as one who serves. "Teach us to search out and to discover in our respective professions the divine meaning," writes a modern Orthodox monk in the same spirit.

"Transform our work into a service and a gift."[47] Such a life means to pray without ceasing and to give thanks for all things. Taking up an Old Testament command, Bukharev invites followers of Christ to "cast aside the Egyptian" (Ex 3:22) which means to convert the idolatrous culture to its true divinohuman calling: worship of the living God through service to others. Enlivened and sanctified by the Spirit, the most humble expression of work becomes noble, and the work of thinker and artist alike become eucharistic offerings of thought and action oriented toward a constant goal of the final accomplishment when God will be all in all.

In the middle of this luminous vision stands the victorious cross of our Savior. This spirituality of compassionate love and celebration to which all the confessors of faith in Christ are invited is not an easy path. It is an engagement that exposes its adherents to criticisms, anger, and mockery. It requires a state of liberating detachment and poverty of spirit that purifies relationships with everything and everyone, free will for the choice of total consecration and interior peace, the fruit of spiritual combat. This peace comes not from avoiding temptations but rather from facing them squarely. In and through struggles of water and fire, the Lord leads his elect.[48]

NOTES

1. Nikolai Berdiaev, "Sources and Meaning of Russian Communism" in the collection *Idées* (Paris: 1963), p. 95.

2. Much of Bukharev's correspondence which I have translated appears in *Alexandre Boukharev: Un Théologien de l'Église Orthodoxe Russe en dialogue avec le monde moderne* (Paris: Beauchesne, 1977). [Ed. note: This is Elisabeth Behr-Sigel's doctoral dissertation.]

3. Some of Bukharev's rarest works can be found in the special libraries of Paris, particularly in the School of Living Eastern Languages and at the St Sergius Institute. An unpublished text by Bukharev recently appeared in the theological review of the Moscow Patriarchate, *Bogoslovskie Trudy*, no. 9, 1972.

4. Cf. Paul Evdokimov, *Le Christ dans le pensée russe,* (Paris: Cerf, 1970), pp. 85-89. See also Elisabeth Behr-Sigel, "An Orthodox Prophet," *Contacts*, no. 82, 1973.

5. *Theological Messenger,* April-May 1917, p. 523 (in Russian).

6. This conversation was reported by Bukharev himself, in an unpublished autobiography written just before he died, entitled "My Hero" (in Russian, *Moi Geroi*). This text was published in the appendix of Bukharev's *Memoire* edited by M. P. Pogodin in *Sbornik sluzhashchii dopolneniem Prostoi Riechi* (Moscow: 1875). Anna Bukhareva also published it in *Svobodnaia Sovest I,* Moscow, 1906.

7. P. Znamensky, a historian of the Kazan Academy and the first biographer of Bukharev, identifies this Pauline verse as the scriptural foundation of Bukharev's theology.

8. Since the reform of theological studies under Alexander I in the beginning of the nineteenth century, the Moscow Church Academy has been housed in the Holy Trinity Monastery.

9. The circumstances under which he made this decision were narrated to Fr Valerien Lavrski, a friend and disciple, by Bukharev himself. In order to intervene in Bukharev's anxious questioning about his vocation, the elder advised him to pray for God's guidance and then open the Bible to the Psalms and the first verses he came to would reveal God's will. Alexander did this and read, "Offer a sacrifice to God and pay your vows to him" (Ps 76:12). He was dismayed, though he had no doubt that God was calling him to a monastic vocation.

10. Letter to Alexander Dubrovsky, *Theological Messenger*, April-May, 1917, p. 564 (in Russian).

11. These details were taken from "Material for a Biography" assembled by Anna Bukhareva in *Svobodnaia Soviest*, Moscow, 1906 (in Russian).

12. Letter of September 20, 1863, to Valerien and Alexandra Lavrski, in Behr-Sigel, *Alexandre Boukharev*, pp. 129-130.

13. *Orthodoxy and the Modern World*, 2nd ed. (St Petersburg: 1906), p. 68 (in Russian).

14. The religious roots of the Russian revolutionary movement were studied by Nikolai Berdiaev, *The Origin of Russian Communism*, and by Nadejda Gorodetzky, *The Humiliated Christ in Modern Russian Thought*.

15. *What is to be done?* is the title of a well-known novel by Chernyshevsky. Lenin later took the same title for one of his books.

16. Pertaining to the spiritual and political mission of St Sergius, cf. P. Kovalevsky, *Saint Sergius and Russian Spirituality* (Crestwood, NY: St Vladimir's Seminary Press, 1976).

17. Cf. *Concerning Orthodoxy*, pp. 58, 60. I use the page references here of the first edition (St Petersburg: 1890).

18. Ibid., p. 59.

19. Ibid., p. 60-61.

20. Bukharev worked for more than twenty years on a *Commentary on the Apocalypse*. He saw it as his life's work. Having been censured for many years, the work was finally published in 1916 by *Sergiev Posad*, thirty-five years after the author's death. By decoding the apocalytic symbolism of St John the Theologian, Bukharev believed he had also determined the signs of the times for his day. From this occasionally doubtful theological foray, some deep spiritual intuitions emerged.

21. Letter to P. V. Lavrski, Sept. 20, 1863. "The Letters of Archimandrite Feodor to his friends in Kazan" was published in the *Theological Messenger* of the Moscow Adacemy (in Russian).

22. Cf. *Concerning Orthodoxy*, p. 3.

23. Ibid., p. 5.

24. On this subject, see also P. Znamensky, *A Theological Polemic in the 1860's* (Kazan: 1902) (in Russian).

25. Cf. note 19 above.

26. The text of Archimandrite Feodor's requests to the Holy Synod are presented in the journal *Russkaia Starina*, vol. 89, 1897. In this text, the monk explains his decision.

27. The decision had many consequences for Bukharev, including the loss of his academic titles, and many restrictions, including the loss of freedom to live in any place where he had exercised his monastic vocation or taught, etc.

28. Letter to professor Gorsky, the future dean of the Moscow Academy, published in the appendix of S. Smirnov's *History of the Moscow Church Academy* (Moscow: 1879) (in Russian).

29. Bukharev makes reference several times to the theme of the monk going into the world, even into unsavory places in order to save a soul—a classic theme of ancient "monastic stories."

30. Letter of July 26, 1862, in Behr-Sigel, *Alexandre Boukharev*, pp. 121-123.

31. *Concerning Orthodoxy*, 2nd ed., pp. 40-47.

32. The totality of the documents concerning the canonical procedure can be found in the Archives of the State of the former Soviet Union in St Petersburg.

33. Letter to P. V. Lavrski, Aug. 2, 1863. The entire text is cited in the appendix. In another letter written to the same person a few years earlier, Feodor cited John 2:27 and held that the prophetic authority of Christ was founded on his willing sacrifice. [Ed. note: at his ordination, the new priest is given part of the eucharistic host, or "Lamb," to hold with the words cited here by Bukharev.]

34. *Theological Messenger*, April-May 1917, pp. 539-540.

35. Paul Evdokimov, *op. cit.*, p. 87.

36. In the Orthodox Church, the sacrament is often referred to as "crowning." Bukharev also sees in this the "crowning" of his new commitment.

37. "Preface" to the 2nd ed., *Concerning Orthodoxy* (St Petersburg, 1906), p. 21.

38. Paul Evdokimov, *Le Christ dans la pensée russe*, p. 89.

39. Elisabeth Behr-Sigel, *The letters of Archimandrite Feodor to Archpriest Valerian Lavrski and to Alexander Lavrski*, doctoral thesis.

40. Nikolai Berdiaev wrote the most "socialist" of his works, dedicated to the memory of Karl Marx, *Christianity and Class War* (Paris, 1932).

41. Among the French Orthodox, we must name Fr Lev Gillet, better known by his pseudonym, "A Monk of the Eastern Church." He wrote many works on spirituality.

42. *Contacts*, no. 51, 1965, a special issue devoted to Mother Maria.

43. Lev Gillet, "Paul Evdokimov, Worshipper in Spirit and Truth," *Contacts*, no. 73-74, 1970.

44. First published in Lyons in 1946, later under the title *The Sacrament of Love* (Crestwood, NY: St Vladimir's Seminary Press, 1985).

45. Crestwood, NY: St Vladimir's Seminary Press, 1998.

46. The continuity of this evangelical thread in Russian Orthodox spirituality was brought to light by the Russian historian George Fedotov, and then subsequently by Elisabeth Behr-Sigel in her book, *Prayer and Holiness in the Russian Orthodox Church* (Paris, 1950).

47. A Monk of the Eastern Church, *They Will Look to Him* (Chevetogne, 1975), pp. 79-80.

48. Letter to Alexandra Lavrskaia, June 18, 1861, published in the *Theological Messenger*, 1917, p. 563.

7

The Bible, Tradition, the Sacraments: Sources of Authority in the Church*

At this moment of meeting together at Bossey, for the third seminar devoted to common reflection on the questions that women pose to the churches today—questions to which they give varying replies, or none at all—there has just begun at Graz, not far from here, a great assembly organized by the European churches on the theme of reconciliation. On the practical level, it was unforeseen. I think the coincidence has deprived us here of the presence of Teny Pirri Simonian, one of the principal organizers of these Bossey seminars, as well as Beate Stierle.

In spite of the inconvenience, though, I am delighted at the coincidence, which has a profound significance for me. Our seminars here at Bossey and the Graz assembly share the same basis. Both of them, under different forms, are the expression of the same great aspiration: an aspiration toward the unity of the people of God, toward overcoming the tensions and conflicts that hinder the fullness of communion—the *koinonia*—that, according to an eminent Orthodox theologian, Metropolitan John Zizioulas, constitutes the essence of the "ecclesial being," the Church as the matrix of a humanity reconciled with God and reconciled within itself according to its divine vocation.

I hope, then, that the thinking of the Graz assembly will be with us during these coming days. We should ask God's blessing on it, and our reflection and discussion here should endorse the assimilation and manifestation of the great reconciliation that is already given in Christ, according to the apostle Paul's epistle to the Galatians: "As many of you as have been baptized into Christ have put on Christ. There is neither Jew nor Greek, there is neither bond nor free, there is neither male nor female: for you are all one in Christ Jesus" (3:27-28).

---

* Adapted from a paper read at the Bossey Seminar, "Authority and the Community of Women and Men in the Church," June 23 to July 3, 1997.

This seminar that brings us together is the third in a series that began in 1992. I have had the privilege and the joy of taking part in the two previous ones, and here I am among you again, although I have the feeling I'm due to be pensioned off. These seminars—as we see from the preparatory text for this one—aspire to be a place, a forum for constructive, loyal, and irenic dialogue about theological problems concerning the questions put by women to the Church, to the various churches. In reality, arising in the context of an immense and profound cultural mutation—a mutation most strongly affecting the West, although it has become a worldwide phenomenon—this questioning receives different replies within the various Christian communities. Most especially over the question of the openness to women of ministries conferred by a specific blessing or sacramental ordination, the Orthodox and Roman Catholic churches on one side, and the majority of the churches resulting from the Protestant Reformation on the other, have adopted positions that are not just different but are in apparent opposition to one another. With the Protestants, women today are admitted to a presbyteral ministry and, although more rarely, to the episcopate or its equivalent, a possibility from which the great traditional churches, as well as certain Protestant communities reckoned as "fundamentalist," consider themselves debarred. The problem of the ordination of women and, along with it, the women themselves have in this way during the last several decades erupted into ecumenical dialogue, a dialogue that originally appeared essentially to be the preserve of Christians of the male sex. (Do we need to be reminded that, at the Congress on Faith and Order, held in Lausanne in 1927—the seed of the future World Council of Churches that was to be founded twenty years later—there were to be found, among hundreds of male theologians, just six women?) Put forward with timidity from this founding period onward, the problem of the ordination of women has arisen again today as an obstacle to the mutual recognition of ministries. In fact it has replaced in importance many of the ancient oppositions—some of which are in process of being overcome—that were once the greatest stumbling-blocks over which aspirations to unity foundered. In ecumenical circles, the resulting blockage to the unity of his disciples desired and implored by Christ, "that the world may believe" (Jn 17:21), is evident. But it is not mentioned in the official ecumenical dialogues, as we hear from a young Lutheran theologian, Elisabeth Parmentier, in a brilliant doctoral thesis that she recently defended before a jury that included an Orthodox theologian.[1] Silence is kept for fear of arousing passionate responses.

Must we resign ourselves to this impasse? Or could we, dare we, try to find a way through it, and this, without falling into doctrinal relativism, but perhaps allowing different practices in relation to differing historical and cultural contexts, thanks to the deepening of biblical, theological and anthropological premises that have resulted in different positions, thanks to a better perception of the essentials that unite us, and thanks above all to a better reciprocal understanding? It is in this perspective of a fertile theological dialogue, being at the same time both rigorous and open, that these Bossey seminars are placed, especially this third seminar on the theme of "Authority and the Community of Women and Men in the Church."

Before opening our reflection on this theme—because what I have to say constitutes only a modest jumping-off point for the collective reflection that must develop—I think it would be worthwhile to make a fairly lengthy digression.

In the letter in which she invited me to take part in the seminar that has brought us together at this moment, Teny Pirri Simonian referred to the Sheffield Congress of July 1981, organized jointly by the WCC and the Faith and Order Commission on the theme of "The Community of Women and Men in the Church." The idea was, she suggested in her letter, to "revisit Sheffield." Upon thinking about it, it seemed to me that this invitation and suggestion were not only for me, as a witness and relic of this important ecumenical event, but through me, for us all. Our seminar, and I would say our three Bossey seminars, make up a part of the continuity of study, of which the Sheffield Congress sixteen years ago was the result and the crown. It is good and right for us to be aware of this continuity, to "revisit Sheffield," to reread the texts produced by that Congress, to relive the event in order to draw inspiration from it, but also to learn from what, in my opinion, was a check, or a half-check, in Sheffield on the level of ecumenical dialogue.

The Sheffield Congress on "The Community of Women and Men in the Church" was preceded and prepared for at length (from 1978 to 1981) by a study with the same title. The coordinator of this work was a Lutheran theologian, my friend Constance Parvey. The object of this study was not directly the problem of the ordination of women. But this problem could not but be a part of the substratum during a period in which it played a negative part in bilateral dialogue between various churches, such as the dialogue between the Orthodox and Anglican churches, and the internal life of many of the churches that were members of the WCC, such as the Swedish church and the Church of England, which also touched the Catholic Church represented in the Faith and Order Commission. The goal of this preparatory study, as that of the Congress, was to place the problem of the ordination of women—the tip of the iceberg—in its larger theological, ecclesiological, and anthropological context. This, then, seems to me also to be the aim of our seminars.

The study launched in 1978 took the form of investigations and publications, but most especially of regional or thematic consultations, the former intended as a sounding of Christian opinion in various large global regions, including Europe, America, the Middle East, and Asia, and the latter to explore the terrain. This was the aim of the consultation at Klingenthal in Alsace on the ordination of women, and that at Nieder-Altaich in Austria on theological anthropology. The Congress itself was composed of plenary sessions and a great many workshops on different themes very similar to the ones with which we are engaged here: "The Authority of the Scriptures," "The Scriptures in the New Community of Women and Men," "Ministry and Worship in the New Community," "Authority and Institutional Structures in the New Community." We see echoes of this work of reflection in the *Sheffield Report*, published in English by the WCC in 1983, a book that is a precious source of information.

Given a mandate by the Orthodox Interepiscopal Committee in France, I was privileged to be associated with the whole process, both the preparatory study and the Congress itself, at which (and it was a great honor) I was invited to speak on the Tradition of the Orthodox Church as a source of inspiration in the building of a new community of women and men.

I retain a profound memory of this whole experience. My book, *The Ministry of Women in the Church*, with its hesitations and questions, its pros and cons concerning the ordination of women, is to a great extent the fruit of Sheffield. I like to believe that it bears the mark of the pentecostal climate of Sheffield, of the ferment of ideas and the freedom of speech and of spirit that were evident there. But with the memory of this experience that was for me so rich, there is mixed the sadness of a hitch on the level of ecumenical dialogue: a hitch in particular in the dialogue between the Orthodox and western Christians (or, at least, the bearers of western culture), the former seeing themselves as defenders of the authentic ecclesial Tradition and the latter striving toward a renewal of Church life in which, for many of them, the ordination of women appeared to be the seed and the symbol. This desire was expressed with a great deal of moderation, with a light and modest touch, in the "Recommendations" at Sheffield and very much more passionately in the famous "Letter from Sheffield to the Churches" presented by its authors as a message from the Holy Spirit. Sent to the Central Committee of the WCC that met in Dresden, in August 1981, the Recommendations and the Letter of Sheffield were received, to say the least, coldly by the bishops representing the Orthodox churches. There were some voices raised. Then the curtain fell. In practice, the Recommendations, which, whatever their imperfections, should have provoked a common reflection, were ignored by the Orthodox churches, notably by those of Eastern Europe, the most important from the point of view of the number of their believers.

The reasons for this lack of communication are manifold, and responsibility is certainly shared. It is partly explained by the political context: the climate of the Cold War, and the attendant isolation of the Orthodox churches of the East that were tolerated by the totalitarian Communist regimes only as relics of the past, and as such confined to a liturgical ghetto and denied free speech. A cultural abyss separated them from Christians of the western churches, free churches seized by a modernity and the challenges to which they believed themselves called to respond. The debate on the ordination of women was of no interest to the Orthodox churches that were struggling for their very survival. It seemed to them to be "unreal," as Fr Alexander Schmemann, one of the few Orthodox theologians to take this debate seriously, wrote at the time. On their side, western partisans of the ordination of women took little account of the opposition of the Orthodox, reckoning that they could easily sweep it aside. As Constance Parvey admitted in the *Sheffield Report*, they were incapable of listening to the Orthodox and made no effort to understand them.

If I have paused a little on this negative element, it is not in order to accuse anyone but because I am convinced that today, in a new context, young Christians—Orthodox, Protestant, and Catholic—are called to resume the dialogue that has been to some extent lost by the "oldies," of whom I am one. It is a matter of taking up the thread again, of returning to Sheffield to find the themes, avoiding the mistakes and sins of their predecessors: self-sufficiency and ignorance of the other that is so often a form of disdain.

Finishing the digression, I shall come ("at last!" you may say) to the theme given to us for our consideration: the Bible, Tradition, and the sacraments, sources of authority for the Church. It is abundantly clear that the term "Church" here signifies the Church as a historical institution, a structured community of humans in which certain people exercise functions of authority. There arises here a vast subject for meditation: what is the true Church? What is the relationship between that which I would call the spiritual essence of the Church, the Church in the mind and eternal intention of God, and the Church on earth, the people of God called to live within the movement of history? From the point of view of Orthodox ecclesiology, these two aspects of the Church are at the same time distinct and interactive. In his book entitled *The Orthodox Church*, a work that is still a relevant text, Fr Sergius Bulgakov, who was something of a modern Origen in the Orthodox Church, writes at length on this subject. His book opens with the sentence: "Orthodoxy is the Church of Christ on earth. The Church of Christ is not an institution; it is new life with Christ and in Christ, guided by the Spirit."[2] And a few pages further on: "We cannot define the limits of the Church, either in space or in time, or in the power of action. The depths of the Church cannot be plumbed." But he adds, "This does not render the Church invisible, in the sense of not existing on earth in a form accessible to experience. No, although the Church's existence is hidden from us, it is visible on earth... it has its limits in time and space. The invisible exists in the visible, it forms part of it; they together form a symbol... it is the unity of the transcendent and the immanent, a bridge thrown across between heaven and earth. From this point of view, the life of the Church, its mysterious life hidden beneath visible signs, is symbolic."[3] I have quoted this text of Fr Bulgakov because the tension between the transcendent and the immanent aspects of the Church, between the eternal and the temporal, and also the importance of symbolism, seem to me to be characteristic of the Orthodox conception and perception of the Church.

It is within the heart of this vision of the Church as a symbolic reality, a divine-human reality, the anticipation of the kingdom of God that both is and is to be, that we as Orthodox approach the question of the exercise of authority in the Church, of the source and the foundation of this authority, of structures of authority that need modifying in order to respond to the challenges of history and to make the exercise of authority conform more closely to the spirit of the Gospel.

A preliminary question. What do we mean by "authority"? And what does it mean "to be invested with authority"? The notion of authority is close to that of power, of might, although it carries an important nuance. In the encyclopedia that I have consulted, it is defined as "legitimate or legal power," or as the "right" to command. Different from brute force, authority has to do with relationships between people, between thinking subjects, who test their opinions and produce balanced judgments. We speak of the force of a hurricane, but not of its authority. Authority is authority only to the extent to which it is accepted and recognized, even by one who repudiates it.

For the Christian, supreme authority belongs to God revealed in his Son on whom the Spirit of the Father rests: one God in three persons, whose being, whose common nature, is love. All authority in the Church comes from him and is exercised in his name: in the name of God transcendent who speaks to humans, who reveals himself to them and gives them his gifts, the gift of his own life: a treasure that we have, as the apostle Paul writes, "in earthen vessels" (2 Cor 4:7). It is in this tension between the divine and human aspects of the authority with which some people are invested in the Church that we find, at one and the same time, the nobility and difficulty of its exercise.

According to the first account in the Bible of the creation of the human couple (Gen 1:27-31), man and woman, created equally in God's image, are called upon to rule over the earth. Together they bear the authority that comes from God the creator. This story was meditated on at length by the Fathers of the Church, the founders of Christian anthropology, an anthropology that is not androcentric, i.e., centered on the male as certain feminists assume, but theocentric, centered on the idea that humanity in its true nature is turned toward communion with God. An orientation common to man and woman, obscured and misled but not destroyed by sin, it was restored in Christ the God-man through communion with him. Speaking in his *The Origin of Man* to a woman who seemed to doubt that this dignity was shared by women and men, St Basil the Great of Caesarea hurled this challenge at her: "Woman, like man, is in the image of God. You have therefore become like God by your goodness in loving others and your brothers, in loathing evil and overcoming the sinful passions, and you therefore have the power to command."[4]

The traditional churches and the Orthodox churches in particular have never taught that Christian women, because they are women, are deprived of the authority that through baptism belongs to every one of Christ's disciples. Together with baptism, Christians in the traditional churches have always received the sacrament of chrismation, the sacrament of the gift of the Holy Spirit, the sign of becoming one of the holy people, a chosen race, a royal priesthood, according to 1 Peter 2:9. Obscured and forgotten, the notion of the royal priesthood of all the baptized, both men and women, has always existed in the depths of the Church, even though it was the "treasure hidden in the field" of the Gospel parable. The personal, spiritual authority of certain women has always been recognized: messengers of Christ's resurrection, confessors of the faith, martyrs, consecrated virgins, nuns, and also evangelists like St Nina of Georgia and St Thekla; simple laywomen sharing the ordinary life of women, married women and mothers of families, as was Juliana Lazarevskaya in Russia on the eve of modern times. Women have been venerated as saints. Mary, the mother of Jesus, is given the titles Queen and Sovereign Lady.

At the same time, however, we must admit that women have progressively, almost from the beginning of Christianity, been kept aside from the functions or ministries that give an institutional form of authority. Except within certain dissident groups such as the Montanists, they have not had access to the ministry of the priesthood or diaconate. They were forbidden to teach, at least within the framework of public worship. During the same period in the fourth century, Basil of Caesarea, who saw his sister Macrina as his spiritual mother, called upon women on the basis of the account in Genesis to be aware of their dignity as daughters of God.⁵ At this same time another Father of the Church, Epiphanius of Salamina, elaborated and developed the doctrine according to which, in the Church, only Christians of the male sex could accede to the priesthood in the measure to which it is a function of authority. He did this basing himself on Tradition, which for him was immutable, and on the teaching of Holy Scripture that proclaims woman's inferiority and the necessity of her submission to man, according to the divine will. "Never from the foundation of the world," affirms Epiphanius, "has a woman served the Lord as priest." This "never" clearly refers to Old Testament tradition, as Epiphanius could not have been ignorant of the existence of priestesses in pagan cults. Tertullian, one of the Latin Fathers of the Church, expresses a similar opinion. "Women are not permitted to speak in church, nor to teach, nor to offer the sacrifice, nor to aspire to any function reserved to men," he affirms, standing against the pretensions of certain women to confer baptism. We find the same interdiction in the *Apostolic Constitutions*, a canonical collection from the end of the fourth century. The right to baptize implies that women have access to the authority that, according to the cosmic orders and confirmed by the Bible, is the province of men only. "In fact," we read, "if, according to 1 Corinthians 11:3, 'the head of the woman is the man,' and it is the latter who is designated for the priesthood, it would never be right to overturn the created order and abandon the chief, the head, to go to the body's extremity."[6] Elsewhere, and even more frequently used, we find the Pauline image of the Church, the body of Christ, to make woman the symbol of sinful humanity saved by Christ while man is called to represent the Savior and proclaim his message of grace.

Ever since the first centuries of Christianity, there has been this tension between two anthropologies. The first affirms that men and women, while different, are equal before God in dignity, sharing in different ways in the same essential responsibility for the doing of his will. The other is the one that sees in woman not necessarily a despicable being, but a being subject to the benevolent and protective authority of the man, this being in the perspective that Elisabeth Moltmann designated at Sheffield as the gentle patriarchalism that is rejected by women today.[7] The tension between these two anthropologies runs through the Bible and the whole of the Church's history. In practice, through the centuries, within patriarchal cultures, it is the latter that has prevailed. But it is questioned today through a different reading of the Bible and a different vision of the Tradition by virtue of a newness that could, in reality, be a return to the sources, an unceasing discernment in the renewal of the eternal Gospel of Christ, of the essential message beneath the historical dust and slag that cover it.

It is in the perspective of this new view of the Bible and of Tradition that our consideration during this seminar is placed. We ask ourselves what the basis of the authority of the Bible is for us, for Christians. Is it for us a sort of fetish fallen from the sky, or maybe a code, an encyclopedia that we only need open to such-and-such a page to find the answer to our present questions about the ordination of women? Is it, for us, the bearer of the living word of God, the divine word which must be perceived through human words and languages conditioned by historical cultures? Does this contextualization of biblical texts, in the way in which it is handled by modern scientific exegesis, ruin the authority of Holy Scripture? Is it, or is it not, in contradiction to the holy Tradition of the Church, to the traditional reading and interpretation of Scripture? The question also arises: what is Tradition? Is it, as one brilliant Protestant woman theologian said at Sheffield, "a collection of hopes that belong to the past," something that needs to be superseded, or, on the contrary, as I attempted to say at the same

Congress, is authentic Tradition "the life of the Church itself, both in its creativity and in its continuity, and in its ever burgeoning newness?" "From
ancient wells," as my friend Archimandrite Lev Gillet said, "we can draw
out a water that is forever fresh and new." Is the Church's Tradition in its
essence an emotion (in the strongest sense of the word), a self-propagating
dynamism for us? How can we distinguish the authentic, living Tradition of
the Church from the traditions, in the plural, that are not bad in themselves
but are relative to their historical situation?

As a corollary, what is our conception of the sacraments? In particular,
for us Orthodox and for our Catholic and Protestant brethren, what is our
conception of the sacrament of ordination as the source of the authority
exercised in the Church by some, by those we call "ministers," that is to
say, in the correct meaning of the word, "servants?" Does the sacramental
conception of ecclesial ministry exclude women? Does sacerdotal ordination, radically distinct from a simple blessing, confer on the recipient, who
can only be a human being of the male sex, a "divine power?" Does it give
to his words and his gestures an efficacy, ex opere operato, in some way
magical? Or is it the consecration and making authentic by the Church of
a personal call that comes from God? Is the call to specific service in the
Church—with the imploring, confident in Christ's promise, of the gifts of
the Holy Spirit—demanded for the good exercise of the authority implied
in this service?

These are serious questions. I do not pretend to have answers for all of
them. My aim here is only to introduce, to be the prologue to a discussion
that will, we hope, allow us to clarify our position, to understand each
other better and to move toward that unity in the essentials of the faith in
the diversity of our cultural traditions that has been the goal envisaged by
the WCC ever since its formation.

I shall restrict myself, in conclusion, to several remarks that might eventually serve as a jumping-off point for a discussion that could deepen them.

My point of view is that of an Orthodox woman theologian who is
attempting to give an account of her faith, of the faith of the Church to
which she belongs, with an attempt to reply to the questions posed by her
Catholic and Protestant brothers and sisters, and to those challenges on
the part of modernity by which we are all confronted. A first group of
remarks concerns the authority of the Scriptures, of the Bible as the living
word of God.

The Orthodox Church is most certainly a biblical church. The Bible, as bearer of the word of God, is treated with reverence. The Gospel book is always placed in the center of the holy table, and the priest, when coming to it, begins by kissing the Gospel book. This could be just a formality, a sort of fetishism. But the Orthodox Church has always encouraged the reading of the holy Scriptures for everyone, even though, as a result of unfavorable historical conditions, private reading has been a rare practice during certain periods. However, certain scriptural texts that have their place in liturgical prayer have profoundly marked and impregnated the piety of the faithful. It is true that the approach to the Bible has been and often remains, though not always, literalist. The Fathers of the Church, however, distinguished between the literal and the spiritual meaning of the Scriptures.

Biblical science and scientific exegesis were born and have developed in the West. They are taught in Orthodox theological schools, even though, for cultural and historical reasons, this contextualization of the Scriptures remains strange to many of the faithful. Resisted by the best theologians, literalism still exists on the practical level, mixed, where women are concerned, with neolithic taboos such as the Old Testament's levitical prescriptions concerning ritual impurity and women's menstruation. They also apply, and this is too often forgotten, to men. We must note, however, that reference to these taboos has more or less disappeared from the Orthodox arguments against the ordination of women. Bishop Kallistos Ware writes that in Christ, who is the fulfillment of the law and the prophets, the word of God made flesh, Old Testament legalism is superseded.

According to Fr John Meyendorff, one of the most eminent contemporary Orthodox theologians,

> The Church, as the community of those who have received the salvation brought by concrete historical events, can have no other foundation than 'the apostles and prophets' (Eph 2:20) who witnessed to 'that which they have heard, which they have seen with their eyes, which their hands have touched (1 Jn 1:1); but this salvation of which they are witnesses has precisely the result of bringing God to live among us and of making the Spirit 'guide us into all Truth' (Jn 16:13).[8]

It is in the Spirit who rested on Christ and who reveals him to us, in the heart of his message, that the Church is called to decipher the sense for her, here and now, of the apostles' witness. Biblical fundamentalism, the literalist interpretation of biblical and New Testament texts isolated from their literary and historical context, must in no way be considered as conforming to the authentic Tradition of the Orthodox Church. I am thinking here of certain Pauline or deutero-Pauline texts such as Ephesians 5:22, "Wives, submit yourselves to your own husbands as to the Lord," or I Timothy 3:12, "I do not permit a woman to teach," texts that must be placed in their historical context.

In conclusion, I want to say a few more words about that faithfulness that must not be confused with an ossified traditionalism. I believe I am here a modest mouthpiece of a whole movement that has, in the course of the twentieth century, renewed and vivified Orthodox theology in consideration of the faith within our churches. The representatives of this movement, theologians of very different thinking in other ways, all insisted on the fact that this indispensable examination of the authentic Tradition of the Church to which they were appealing was not to be identified with a mechanical repetition of the past. Fr Sergius Bulgakov, in his masterful work which was the first exhaustive study on the Orthodox Church to appear in French during the 1930s, writes in words that I have already quoted, "The Church of Christ is new life with Christ and in Christ, guided by the Spirit." And a little further on he writes, "Tradition is not an archeological wall or a dead deposit!"

Tradition is the memory of the past, but this past must be living Tradition, and this, the title of one of his books, is also affirmed by Fr John Meyendorff, a representative of the second generation of the Russian emigration in western Europe and North America and a promoter of a fertile return to the Fathers, the founders of Orthodox theology. He writes,

> dead traditionalism cannot be truly traditional. It is an essential characteristic of patristic theology that it was able to face the challenges of its own time while remaining consistent with the original apostolic Orthodox faith... True tradition is always *living* tradition. It changes while remaining always the same. It changes because it faces different situations, not because its essential content is modified. This content is not an abstract proposition; it is the Living Christ Himself, who said, 'I am the Truth.'[9]

I could quote others, such as my friend Vladimir Lossky, who saw in Tradition the critical spirit of the Church. It allows the Church to discern, in the Holy Spirit, the authentic from the non-authentic, to distinguish the essence of the message of the Gospel from non-essential and therefore ephemeral historical additions. This idea is taken up and developed by Fr John Meyendorff, who denounces the temptation to live in the past, to which the Orthodox too often succumb. Placed in difficult historical conditions, and this has once again been the case very recently, they believe that they must, in order to preserve that which is essential, conserve everything. Fr Meyendorff comments, "And so the legitimate concern for the continuity of the Church's life and respect for Tradition risk degenerating into an ossified conservatism." It is vital that the Orthodox church resist this temptation. And so Meyendorff says in conclusion:

> One of the most basic problems for theologians today is knowing how to discern between the holy Tradition of the Church—an expression adequate or appropriate to Revelation—and the human traditions which express Revelation only imperfectly and, very often, which even oppose and obscure it. How many of these human traditions should the Orthodox abandon before other Christians will accept their claim of having the true and unique Tradition? The merit, that is, the historical merit of the Christian East, is to have largely allowed an open door to such an examination of conscience.[10]

I continue to make this conclusion and this hope my own, as expressed by my friend more than thirty years ago. Will the Orthodox Church be capable of responding to one of the greatest challenges of our time, the desire of women, in accordance with the revolution in the understanding of the Gospel, to be recognized as free and responsible persons, capable of participating in various ways in the responsibilities and consequently the authority exercised in the Church? I hope so. And hope, together with faith and love, is a theological virtue, a grace that we must not cease to implore.

NOTES

1. Cf. Elisabeth Parmentier, "L'Ordination des femmes" (The Ordination of Women), in *Positions luthériennes*, 1997:1.

2. *The Orthodox Church*, rev. trans. Lydia Kesich (Crestwood, NY: St Vladimir's Seminary Press, 1988), p. 1.

3. Ibid., p. 7.

4. *The Origin of Man*, Homily 1:18.

5. On Macrina and her relationship with her brothers Basil of Caesarea and Gregory of Nyssa, see Ruth Albrecht's important doctoral thesis, *Das Leben der heiligen Makrina* (Göttingen,

1986). Her sources on Macrina are her hagiographic "Life," recounted by her brother Gregory of Nyssa, and his *Dialogue on the Soul and the Resurrection*.

6. *Apostolic Constitutions*, 3:9:1-4.

7. *The Community of Women and Men in the Church: The Sheffield Report*, ed. Constance Parvey (Geneva: WCC, 1983), p. 62.

8. *Living Tradition* (Crestwood, NY: St Vladimir's Seminary Press, 1978), p. 15.

9. Ibid., pp. 7-8.

10. *The Orthodox Church: Its Past and Its Role in the World Today*, 4th ed., rev. Nicolas Lossky (Crestwood, NY: St Vladimir's Seminary Press, 1996), p. x.

8

Jesus and Women[*]

From the beginning to the end, from the stable of Bethlehem to Golgotha and to the garden on Easter morning, women are present in Jesus' earthly life. This is the witness of the Gospels. Uncommon in terms of Jewish customs of the day, the presence of women—including some of dubious morals—among those closest to the Galilean was striking for his contemporaries. Jesus' adversaries, the Pharisees, criticized him for it, as is seen in the story of the woman caught in adultery who was brought to him. It discredited him in their eyes. His disciples as well were astonished when they found him in conversation with a woman, who was also a Samaritan, thus considered a heretic (Jn 4:27).

Jesus allowed himself to be touched, both physically and morally, by women: by the woman with a hemorrhage, who was considered impure (Mt 9:18-22) and by the woman who had sinned, who covered his feet with her tears and kisses (Lk 7:36-50). He gave in to the moving pleas of the Canaanite woman (Mt 15:21-28; Mk 7:24-30). From Galilee, he was accompanied by a group of women who "had been cured of evil spirits and infirmities" (Lk 8:2). Among these women, one is always named, while the names of others vary in the different Gospels: Mary called Magdalene, "from whom seven demons had gone out," an intimate friend of Jesus, who would be the first to see the Resurrected One.

For later Christian commentators, the Gospel texts which recall the Lord's numerous relationships with women created a problem. They thought they resolved it by covering what would normally be Jesus' disrepute with pious intentions which justified these dubious associations. Women's miseries—illness, impurity, ignorance, sin—are supposed to have called forth the Savior's infinite mercy. These women represented humanity, totally lost without him. Male human beings, on the other hand, were

* Adapted from the WCC Unit III-Istanbul Consultation, 1997. Edited and revised by Fr Michael Plekon.

chosen to be his apostles, to represent him and to proclaim his message of grace. Nevertheless, the question arises: does such an interpretation, which bears the mark of plain ordinary thousand-year-old androcentrism, stand up to an honest and rigorous examination of the New Testament text? Does it correspond to Jesus' intentions as they are revealed there?

The first thing we notice is that Jesus has relationships with quite a few women. But he never speaks to them as a separate group, characterized neither by vice nor by certain specific virtues. He never denounces the faults usually ascribed to women: weakness, frivolity, coquetry, sensuality, excessive emotionality. Neither does he exalt feminine virtues. Jesus does not exhort women to be obedient and submissive as is proper for them. He does not speak of feminine tenderness as opposed to masculine toughness. I dare say that Jesus is not interested in woman, but rather in women, in each of them as he meets her personally. He enters directly into dialogue with each, deducing her needs and endeavoring to respond to them, to women just as men; to each one personally he addresses the message of grace, the invitation to enter the kingdom of heaven, which is brought near to them in him. He does not see women as a "breed," a category of dangerous and despicable beings. In the words of the Protestant woman theologian, France Quere, through his behavior toward women, "Jesus broke with the myth of Eve as having brought sin into the world, as a woman, and having passed on her evil spells and her guilt to all female posterity."[1]

The Son of God made man is fully human. He who inaugurated his ministry by attending the wedding at Cana, where he changed the water of human joy into the wine of the kingdom of heaven, does not despise sexuality. Jesus is not unaware of the reality of difference between the sexes, but for him, women are not limited by their sexual role. As humans they are, like their male partners, beings endowed with speech: persons. God speaks to them. According to the Orthodox theologian Olivier Clément, the evangelical revolution, at the anthropological level, "is the advent of the person, as opposed to the species simply as a whole, and as opposed to the ecstasies of union."[2]

The Gospels evoke the relationships of Jesus with various women: brief, dazzling encounters, or long, peaceful friendships where the decisive word suddenly breaks in, such as Martha of Bethany's confession of faith (Jn 11:27). Jesus touches the bent-over woman, and she stands straight (Lk 13:10-17). To the widow of Nain he gives back her only son (Lk 11:11-17).

A force or "energy" goes out of him and cures the woman with a hemorrhage who has dared to touch his garment (Mt 9:18-22). Jesus takes the
woman caught in the act of adultery away from the Pharisees who claimed
the right to judge her (Jn 8:1-11). Each time, the miracle—healing, liberation, forgiveness—is accompanied by a saying of Jesus which reveals its deep
meaning. These sayings proclaim the restored dignity of these women as
daughters of Abraham the faithful and direct them toward a new life: "Take
heart, daughter; your faith has made you well" (Mt 9:23); "Neither do I con-
demn you. Go your way, and from now on do not sin again" (Jn 8:11); "Go
in peace," or rather, more exactly translated, "Go toward peace," peace in
the sense of the fullness of life in the kingdom of God (Lk 7:50).

Between Jesus and the women who have accompanied him from Galilee a truly intimate relationship is established. Mary Magdalene bears witness to this. She recognizes the risen Christ—the master and friend who
now looks different—simply by the tone of his voice calling her by name,
"Mary." From this supremely personal encounter, as the Monk of the
Eastern Church has written, "an emotion shines into the world, which still
gives us life."[3]

Several of the women who have followed Jesus since the beginning of
his ministry obviously come from well-to-do circumstances. They are eco-
nomically and morally independent. Jesus does not send them back to
their husbands. We can guess that they provide for the master's material
needs. Thanks to them, the Son of Man has shelter and food, and does not
need to envy the birds of the air and the crows. However, as the case of
Mary Magdalene in particular illustrates, these women's roles are no limited to that of patrons or housekeepers. They are Jesus' disciples and
friends. When he is arrested and condemned to death, they remain faithful to him. Not one of them betrays him. When the apostles scatter and
run away, except for the one "whom Jesus loved," they remain with him
and Jesus' mother, "near the cross,' communing with the Crucified One in
his suffering (Jn 19:25). Though trembling with shock on seeing the empty
tomb, they obey the angel's command to go and tell the news. "Apostles to
the apostles" is what they are called in the Byzantine liturgy, the first messengers of the Resurrection.

Though capable of courageously taking the initiative, these women
believers normally behave in accordance with the Jewish-Hellenic social
customs of their time. Martha and Mary of Bethany, in whose home Jesus

is a familiar guest, serve him according to the rules of hospitality of their society. For them, this service is not at all humiliating. Does not their master call himself the servant of all? Jesus, in accepting their service, nevertheless does not confine women to housekeeping, to cooking and serving at table. He praises Mary when she leaves these duties to her sister, and sits at his feet like a pupil—a student of the Torah—being taught by a rabbi. Can we not see Mary of Bethany as the patron of modern women students of theology? Even so, Martha the housekeeper is not disdained. It is with her that Jesus has the conversation which culminates in Martha's confession of faith, a confession in every way comparable with that of Peter, chief of the apostles. When Jesus proclaims his messiahship, Martha replies, "Yes, Lord; I believe that you are the Christ, the Son of God, he who is coming into the world" (Jn 11:27).

Other women also have profound dialogues with Jesus. Far from being passive receivers of grace, they are awakened by their encounters with him to their own thinking and faith, and are called to be among Jesus' witnesses in the world. Upon the revelation of Jesus' mysteries, they become important and active agents. It was to a woman, the Samaritan whom Jesus met at the ancient well of Jacob, that he entrusted the revolutionary secret of the "worshippers... in spirit and in truth." She then brought this message to the inhabitants of the city of Sychar (Jn 4:1-42).

The dialogue mixed with irony between Jesus and the Canaanite woman—a foreigner, a pagan—who answers him tit for tat leads to the revelation of Christian universalism, beyond the borders of Israel. Admiring the intensity of this pagan's faith, Jesus exclaims, "Woman, great is your faith! Let it be done for you as you wish" (Mt 15:28).

A woman is at the center of the slightly differing accounts in Mark, Matthew, and John of the anointing at Bethany. Who is she? Mary of Bethany, or Mary Magdalene, as some scholars suggest? Or another unknown, anonymous woman? Actually the historical identity of this woman is not important—what is essential is the meaning of her gesture. On the eve of Passover, on his way to celebrate it in Jerusalem, knowing that he will meet his death there, Jesus is at table. The ceremony of the meal is disturbed as he receives from a woman the priestly anointing which, particularly in the context of Matthew's Gospel, serves to consecrate him as king of Israel and at the same time foretells his death (Mt 26:6-13, Mk 14:3-9, Jn 12:1-8).

The unknown woman, or Mary of Bethany in John's Gospel, breaks open an alabaster jar and pours upon Jesus a "perfume," a very costly "ointment of nard," a gesture out of the ordinary, which the male apostles do not understand. According to their petty calculations, this is nothing but a waste, to no purpose. They rebuke the woman. The money she has spent could have been given to the poor. Jesus alone understands her. They are united in a deep communion, the woman and the suffering yet victorious God. "Truly I tell you, wherever the good news is proclaimed in the whole world, what she has done will be told in remembrance of her" (Mk 14:9). In these words we can discern a sort of mysterious correspondence with the "in remembrance of me" of the institution of the Eucharist. Have the historical churches kept this exhortation and meditated on it sufficiently? Has the perfume of this gesture filled our entire house as the Gospel of John says it did in the house of Mary, Martha, and Lazarus?

We cannot speak of Jesus' relationships without remembering Mary, his mother. Too often the Mother of God has been exalted at the expense of her poor sisters, who are pushed back in the direction of the temptress, Eve, by whom came sin and death. To do this is to falsify the meaning of the Scriptures: it is to ignore the words of Jesus, who saw his mother as the image of the true disciple, the prototype of those "who hear the word of God and do it" (Lk 8:21 and 11:27-28; compare with Lk 1:45 and 2:19). But to speak of Mary together with the other women would require another exposition.

NOTES

1. France Quere, *Les Femmes de l'Evangile* (Paris: Editions du Seuil, 1982).
2. Olivier Clément, *L'Oeil de Feu* (Saint-Clément-la Rivière: Fata Morgana, 1994).
3. Archimandrite Lev Gillet, "Jesus lui dit Marie," *Contacts*, no. 100, 1977.

9

Mary and Women*

First a preliminary remark. A year ago, when I was asked to speak at this colloquy, the theme proposed for my presentation was "Mary and Women." Several months later, when I received the program, I noticed that the title had been changed to "Mary and Woman." The substitution of the singular collective for the plural, a substitution that seemed obvious and one which must have been made without thinking that anyone would notice the difference—well, this substitution gave me something to ponder. It has become the trend, in ecclesiastical circles, to discourse ever so seriously about "woman," "the charisms of woman," "her vocation," etc. I must admit having used this form myself in the title of the French version of one of my books.[1] Now to adopt systematically such language in speaking about us, women, is this not to see in us not persons, each singular and unique, but simple specimens or samples of a species defined essentially by its sex? A sex for a long time despised, at least considered inferior.

Today clergy and theologians in the West, perhaps in order to maintain a good conscience about this, often have the tendency to "idealize," to exalt the "charisms of women," which then define for women radically different tasks than those of men.[2] But to make this biological differentiation and then to transpose it into the spiritual domain, is this not to ignore the dignity of *anthropos*, that which distinguishes humanity from the animals among whom, according to the biblical account, Adam did not find one with whom to communicate when he needed, another like him? In the wake of popularized and sublimated Freudianism, the modern avatar of archaic stereotypes, doesn't this obscure the fundamental revolution in the domain of anthropology brought about by the Judaeo-Christian tradition, the "coming of the person over against the play of the species"?[3] "Mysterious, open to the transcendent," the person, neither rejected nor scorned

* Originally published in *Théologie, histoire et piété mariale: Actes du colloque de la Faculté de Théologie de Lyon*, 1 to 3 October 1996, pp. 309-325. Translated by Fr Michael Plekon.

because of sex but transcending it, is affirmed by the theologians of the Orthodox Church in the second half of the twentieth century, those who continue the theological anthropology of the Greek Fathers (especially the Cappadocians and Maximus the Confessor), such figures as Vladimir Lossky, John Meyendorff, Olivier Clément, John Zizioulas, and Verna Harrison. God, one yet in three persons, is the paradigm of created humanity according to the Bible, "in his image and likeness" (Gen 1:26-27). In the image of its creator, humanity is one in the distinction of persons, at the same time equal in dignity and yet ineffably different, capable of communicating, called to commune with respect to the otherness of the other person, the mysterious, indescribable, inexplicable otherness, colored by sex but not reducible to sexual difference.

I apologize for this preamble, seemingly outside the subject at hand, but I believed it necessary to make precise the anthropological perspective in which I situate this modest contribution reflecting on the meaning, for women, of the image of Mary, mother of Jesus, mother of the Son of God, borne by the Tradition of the Church. What I have said therefore needs to be deepened, completed, and perhaps rectified.

"Mary and women." The very statement of this theme raises several questions. First, why should such an inquiry even be pursued? Is it only because of the fact of their sex that Christians who are women have some privileged relation with the Virgin Mary, the mother of God? Has the role of women been decisive in the spread of veneration for Mary? Has this veneration contributed to the recognition by the Church and by society— for the two have more often than not been combined—of the dignity of women?

Before thinking through these questions in the light of the witness of the New Testament, there are some historical challenges that must be dealt with first.

In a rapid overview of the history of the Church, it would seem that in the western as in the eastern spheres of Christianity the promoters of marian piety and theology have often, perhaps most often, been men. Cyril of Alexandria was the inspiration for the title *Theotokos*, "mother" or "bearer of God" at the Council of Ephesus in 431. Nicholas Cabasilas, the Byzantine theologian of the fourteenth century and St Seraphim of Sarov in Russia in the nineteenth, St Augustine and St Bernard of Clairvaux, down to the contemporary popes who proclaimed the dogmas of the immaculate conception and assumption of Mary, even St Maximilian Kolbe, the martyr of Auschwitz, and Fr Teilhard de Chardin: all of them were men.

This is not to say that women have had no role whatsoever in the development and spread of marian devotion on the popular level. Certainly they have contributed. One thinks of the women of Ephesus greeting with a torch-lit procession the proclamation of the Council and of the millions of Christian mothers who have taught their children to pray the "Hail Mary," the salutation of the angel addressed to Mary. Nevertheless, even down to our time, one thinks of Christian women prohibited from preaching in the ecclesial assembly of the liturgy and unable to participate in the elaboration of Marian theology. This has been almost exclusively the business of men, of the clergy, who unconsciously perhaps have imprinted upon the theology of Mary their own dreams, their own vision of the ideal woman, a vision they combined with scorn or at the very least the second-class citizenship of real women within societies of a patriarchal form.

Here we can see the ambivalence of a double discourse on Mary and women, one heard in the Church until very recently, which subordinates real women, while placing between them and Mary an incommensurable distance and at the same time exhorting the very same women to be her humble imitators. On the one hand, attention is concentrated upon the maternal virginity of Mary but understood more in its physical than its theological, Christological, and spiritual significance. It makes of Mary an ideal inaccessible to ordinary women, rejecting these in the same blow, on the other hand, with Eve, the seducer and the one seduced, in whose guilt they are seen to share. "Woman is the gate to hell... Every woman should be weighed down with shame at the very thought that she is a woman," affirms Tertullian, a father of the Latin Church, exhorting women to dress modestly as a sign of their grief for the sin of Eve paid for by the death of the Son of God.[4] For one so designated as guilty, it remains only to implore the intercession of the "most pure Mother of God" with a wrathful God, depicted in masculine characteristics. To be sure, in Mary every woman is glorified. But this idealized Mary has nothing in common with ordinary women. Only a virgin consecrated to God in religious life would appear to resemble her. However, this only discredits the physical, conjugal union of a man and a woman, legitimated solely by the necessity of procreation for the perpetuation of the human race. The assimilation of Eve's guilt by women, by which their lowliness accentuates the glory of Mary, has been a distinguishing feature of Christian teaching and life down through the centuries, as theologian Paul Evdokimov asserts: "Between the summit of humanity, the Virgin Mary who is 'beyond compare more glorious than the seraphim' and whose praise rises like a single spire, and incomplete feminine beings, there does not exist, so it appears, a third option. An amazing alienation has established itself in history as a normal situation."[5]

Parallel with this approach, which appears to open an abyss which cannot be bridged between Mary and other women, is another more pedagogical one which is found more frequently in the West, an approach, I think, which brings Mary and women closer together again. But it makes of Mary a model of obedience and submission for all women. As Mary has submitted to the divine will, so her sisters should in their turn submit to all those who represent God, who always seems to possess masculine identity and traits: their fathers, brothers, husbands, and priests. In the second century, St Irenaeus of Lyons said, "What the Virgin Eve put into bondage, the Virgin Mary has freed." But this message of liberation was rarely if ever applied to actual women down through the centuries, at least in their places in society and in the Church. Women have nevertheless carried the freedom with them, receiving it and keeping it in their hearts.

The persistence of a double discourse such as that which I am evoking here down to our own time in the churches where Marian piety is most intense—I mean in the Catholic and the Orthodox Churches—might explain the suspicion with regard to the figure of Mary on the part of those who could be called the pioneers of the movement for the "emancipation" of women. These pioneers were also mostly from the Protestant churches or were agnostics, certainly hostile to Christianity and to the traditional churches. Within the context of a very complex and profound cultural transformation, the situation has changed today. Christian feminists are reclaiming Mary not only to affirm the dignity of women as human beings but in order to promote specifically feminine values, the particular identity of women as opposed to the values and identity of men. To what extent such an aspiration is within the lines of the personalism of the Gospel and the theological anthropology of the Fathers is a question that must be raised.

In the course of the twentieth century, under the influence of diverse factors, political, economic, scientific, but also specifically spiritual, not only the social position of women but their very self-consciousness, *Selbstbewußtsein,* has been profoundly changed. We see this especially in western societies shaped by Christianity. "Today, after a long period of patriarchy, woman seeks to affirm herself as a complete human person, as a free and responsible subject. It is the ferment of the Gospel which is accomplishing this, finally liberating us from ancient pagan structures."[6] With the exception of a very few precursors, the theologians of the traditional churches have taken a very long time to discern this evangelical ferment "present often *incognito* in the feminist movement." Nevertheless, progressively, under the pressure of the feminist movement, a new discourse about women in relationship to Mary is finally being established, even in official ecclesiastical spheres. Its emergence is located in the context of the debate over the possible access of women to the ministries conferred by sacramental ordination, a problem upon which ecumenical dialogue has now stumbled. Would a renewed Mariology enable the formation of a response to the legitimate aspiration of women in keeping with the traditional exclusion of them from priestly ministry?

Such is the intention, it seems to me, undertaken in the apostolic letter *Mulieris dignitatem* of Pope John Paul II, as well as the writing of certain Orthodox theologians such as Paul Evdokimov in France and Fr Thomas Hopko in the United States as well as their followers.[7] *Mulieris dignitatem*, published in the Marian year of 1988, is from this point of view a particularly important text. Here in the letter we are far from the older approach which at once glorified the Virgin and Mother of God while at the same time humiliating women in whom her submissiveness was to be inculcated. Rather, Mary now becomes a symbol of "the mystery of woman," of the mystery of femininity which, far from being synonymous with any deficiency, is lifted up in its richness. This letter, then, is incontestably a break with the former theological approaches to women. If the classic Catholic theological anthropology elaborated by St Thomas Aquinas recognized the essential equality of men and women as human beings, it was, however, limited by its understanding of the order of creation and of the soul as asexual. According to the natural order, woman in her very body was inferior to man. In the eschatological order, equality would not be fully realized except in the resurrection of the dead. The situation of inferiority (*status subjectionis*) of women excludes them in the here and now from the hierarchical priesthood, which signifies a kind of superiority.

Taking the counter-position, *Mulieris dignitatem* exalts femininity in itself through Mary. Far from associating with the idea of lack or imperfection, femininity means plenitude. "The fullness of grace accorded to the Virgin of Nazareth," the letter says, "signifies the fullness of the perfection of the one who is a woman."[8] As the new Eve, Mary is "the new beginning of the dignity of woman, of all women, of every woman."[9] Given the title of "servant," which contains nothing humiliating, Mary "enters the messianic service of her Son,"[10] and this opens to women new, vast perspectives concerning their ministry in the Church and in the world. "It is evident that woman is called to participate in the dynamic, operating structure of Christianity in a way so important that it is not possible to yet discern all of its particularities."[11]

Yet *Mulieris dignitatem*, after *Inter insigniores* (1972), reaffirms the impossibility of ordaining women to the priestly ministry. The decisive argument is not simply the nearly two thousand-year-old tradition. The impossibility of ordaining women results precisely from the sublimated femininity that defines women, that was magnified in Mary and through her in all women. Christ is the bridegroom of the Church. "The symbol of the bridegroom is of the masculine genre. In aspiring to the priesthood, woman makes herself masculine,"[12] thus losing that which is her "richness" and "originality," this "prophetic character which finds in the Virgin Mother of God its highest expression" and through which Mary and with her all women are connected to the Holy Spirit.[13]

Had Pope John Paul II, while preparing *Mulieris dignitatem*, known and read *Woman and the Salvation of the World*, one of Paul Evdokimov's principal books, published in a new edition in 1978 and translated into a number of languages, one of which was Italian? I cannot prove this but I am struck by the common inspiration which joins both texts. The same compassion for women, the same vision of the Mother of God as "archetype of the feminine,"[14] the same care in responding to the aspirations, judged in part legitimate by the feminist movement, and all complete in reaffirming, as John Paul II, the impossibility of ordaining women to the sacerdotal ministry, an essentially masculine function incompatible with "the charisms of women." "Woman is not capable of being priest without betraying herself." It is through her being, her nature, that she is called to accomplish her royal priesthood in conformity with her charismatic state.[15] Differently from John Paul II, who only makes an allusion to it, Orthodox theology pushes quite far the idea of a particular relationship between "the feminine," of which Mary is the archetype, and the Holy

Spirit. "There is a profound link between the Holy Spirit, Divine Wisdom, the Virgin, the feminine," writes Evdokimov, here representing certain perspectives of the "sophiology" of Russian theological thinking.[16] To the hypostatic motherhood of the Spirit corresponds the earthly divine motherhood of the *Theotokos*, to which woman by her spirit-bearing vocation is called to participate in becoming for the masculine person "the guiding image and doorway of the kingdom, through which she awakens in him the taste, the indestructible nostalgia."[17]

Analogous ideas have been developed in a less romantic fashion, more systematically and more polemically as well, by Fr Thomas Hopko, dean of St Vladimir's Orthodox Theological Seminary in Crestwood, New York, in the more aggressive feminist context in America.[18] Fr Hopko's ideas, as those of Paul Evdokimov, are theological opinions, *theologoumena*, and do not enjoy within the Orthodox Church an authority comparable to that of a papal text within the Roman Catholic Church. However, these have been welcomed with sympathy by part of the Orthodox hierarchy and have undergirded the debates during the Interorthodox Consultation at Rhodes in 1988 on the theme of the participation of women in the life of the Church.[19] "The role of women," as the conclusions of the Consultation put it, "can be expressed in the typology 'Eve-Mary,' and in the specific relationship that women have with the work of the Holy Spirit."[20] Paradoxically, this privileged relationship with the Holy Spirit excludes them, along with Mary, from the priestly ministry which is located within the economy of Christ. Yet these very conclusions affirm in conformity with the constant teaching of the Church that the sacramental priesthood of some persons constitutes a particular charism of the Spirit. I do not intend to enter here into this confused debate, in which the contradictions reveal the lack of clarity and agreement of many Orthodox theologians in the face of what is for them a new and serious problem within ecumenical dialogue, that of the ordination of women to the priesthood.[21]

Apparently gratifying to women, and associated with the idea of a kind of femininity sublimated in the Holy Spirit, the exaltation in Mary of the feminine charisms is attractive to many. But is this not a misunderstanding? To make of femininity something of the essence of Mary, to see in her only the archetype of the feminine, is this not to diminish it? She is a woman, but above all a human being in fullness, in whom, as Maximus the Confessor very powerfully says, "the division between man and woman is surpassed."[22] To perpetuate and even sacralize this separation in placing Mary above all other women, next to the Holy Spirit, with men at the side of Christ: such speculation is in utter contradiction with the baptismal hymn in the epistle to the Galatians (3:26-28) and has no scriptural foundation whatsoever. In practice, feminists point out, such thinking only serves to separate idealized women from any functions which in the Church would imply authority and decision-making.

Who is Mary, according to basic Christian teaching, founded on the witness of the New Testament? The most ancient testimony to her in the New Testament is found in Paul's Epistle to the Galatians. He situates Mary within the history of salvation, a history in which, according to the Judaeo-Christian perspective, a completely transcendent God is the principal actor, but a God *philanthropos*, the lover of mankind, who loves and respects his creatures and wants to bring men and women together. "When the fullness of time had come, God sent his Son, born of a woman" (Gal 4:4). Mary is not a feminine divinity. She is the completely human mother of God who, in order to save humanity not as a *deus ex machina* but from within it, assumes all of humanity. In witness to his full humanity, the Son of God and God-man was born of a woman, according to the reciprocity-equality underscored by Paul, in order to end a very involved debate. "However in the Lord, though woman is nothing without man, man is nothing without woman; and though woman came from man [an allusion to the second account of the creation of the human pair and to its rabbinical interpretation] so does every man come from a woman, and everything comes from God" (1 Cor 11:11-12).

This woman, this human being whom the transcendent God has wished to need in order to realize his plan of love, is not merely a passive instrument in his hands. Her obedience is not blind. Her obedience is that of a free woman, inspired by a total faith, but a faith in search of understanding. This is how Nicholas Cabasilas, the great Byzantine spiritual master of the fourteenth century, emphasized the account of the annunciation in St Luke's Gospel. "When God decided to bring into the world his first-born Son to renew humanity by making of him the second Adam, he had the Virgin share in his plan. God made this serious decision but the Virgin ratified it; the incarnation of the Word was not only the work of the Father, of his Word and of the Holy Spirit... it was also the work of the will and the faith of the Virgin." Cabasilas underscores the freedom of Mary in her clinging to divine will. "Mary conceived by her own will and became the mother of God by a free choice, for in order to share in the plans of God, she could not be a mere tool in the hands of the artist but she offered her very self and thus became a co-worker with God for the salvation of the human race." Mary is not just the body through whom the Word passed in order to become flesh. It was with her entire being, body, soul, will, and intelligence that she participated in the divine mystery of the incarnation of the Son of God, "becoming mother of the body and of the soul, and bringing forth the whole of man in this ineffable giving birth."[23]

According to the Gospel of St Luke, immediately after the annunciation Mary went "in haste" to her relative Elizabeth, who in her old age had conceived a son from her union with the priest, Zechariah. This visitation had a profound meaning. The meeting between Mary and Elizabeth—in which the one who was from God recognized the other, also from God, and leapt for joy—this was a prefiguring of John the Baptist and Jesus. Yet this was also an encounter between two women who had a secret to keep. Her unique vocation did not keep Mary away from other women with whom she shared solidarity. The daughters of Abraham, Mary and Elizabeth, were in communion both in faith and in the accomplishment of the divine promises given to them, as well as in the joy of the messianic kingdom approaching, which would be the taking down of the mighty from their thrones and the exaltation of the lowly, among these latter certainly women. The *Magnificat* of Mary in which Elizabeth is also involved is thus a song of hope.

In Mary, the motherhood of women is sanctified and glorified. This understanding corresponds to a deep intuition and is absolutely correct, but her condition should not be reduced just to her physical maternity and the vocation of women, not simply identified with motherhood. Otherwise men would be deprived of the symbolic richness that Mary offers them.

It is directly against such a misunderstanding that Jesus' words at first risk a shock to those devoted to Mary, his mother. A woman in the crowd called out, "Blessed is the womb that bore you and the breasts that nursed you." And to this Jesus replied, "More blessed are those who hear the word of God and keep it" (Lk 11:27-28; see also Lk 8:21 and the parallels in Matthew and Mark). These words do not denigrate Mary, presented precisely by Luke as the one "who has believed" (Lk 1:45). They illumine the reality that it is the integrity of her faith which for Jesus is the greatness of his mother. The Mother of God by the consent of her faith had a unique vocation which is described as a "sword that will pierce her soul." Mary is the figure of the true disciple, the model of the demanding *sequela Christi*, the following after Christ, to which every person, man and woman, is called.

The Fourth Gospel is distinguished by the attention given by its author to the women who believed in Jesus, such as Mary and Martha of Bethany, Mary Magdalene, and the Samaritan woman at Jacob's well. John's Gospel also lets us see into the relationships between Mary and these women disciples of the Lord. According to the Johannine account of the passion, Mary was present at the foot of the cross where she agonized over her son, with the sister of her mother, Mary, the wife of Cleopas, and Mary Magdalene. Not far away was "the disciple whom Jesus loved." United in sorrow, united in the sharing of the passion of her son the master, Mary, the women, and the disciple represent the Church which until the end of time is united to the offering of Christ "on behalf of all and for all," in the words of the liturgy of the Eastern Church. Seeing his mother and close to her the disciple whom he loved, Jesus said to her, "Woman, behold your son." And to the disciple he said, "Son, behold your mother." The intuition of the Church has always seen in these words something else than the meaning to these individuals. It is the entire gathering of believers, men and women, which is the Church catholic, that Jesus entrusts to his mother and it is all of these, men and women both who believe in him, that constitute his true family whom he asks to receive, that is to say, into their lives, the one who is his mother, the sister of them all.

According to the New Testament, the end of the earthly life of Mary is shrouded in mystery. Mary enters the pentecostal life of the Church. "The life of Pentecost in Mary is eternally contemporary," writes a modern Orthodox spiritual teacher.[24] The faith in her ascending death and transfiguration has been imposed upon believing Christians. Like the Catholic Church, the Orthodox churches celebrate the feast often called "Assumption," but the Orthodox call it instead the "Dormition" or falling asleep of the Mother of God, insisting on her natural death so intimately connected with the mystery of her bodily resurrection and her entry into divine glory.[25]

For Christian consciousness, the assumption of Mary does not mean the glorification of her femininity, that of the "eternal woman." An eschatological sign above and beyond history, she announces and anticipates the end, the meaning or *telos* for which humanity as a whole was created, namely the glorification of the creature when all is accomplished and completed, when God is "all in all."

Mary, in basic Christian perspective, even if popular piety sometimes produces a deformation, is not a feminine divinity, the protectress of women, the sweet and merciful one in contrast to a God presented in masculine form as a harsh judge. She is the human mother of God made man who said himself, "I am meek and humble of heart," meekness and humility being for the patriarchal society in which he said these words, essentially feminine characteristics. She is the servant of the God who is "boundless love," who reveals himself as the supreme servant, the slave of all. To make of Mary, as some para- or post-Christian currents of feminist theology would have it, a "Goddess," a projection of feminine aspirations and values, a divinity who permits women to realize themselves without becoming like "God," that is male—such would be to return to a very ancient paganism, simply in modern dress.

In addressing his mother, Jesus called her "woman." Mary is a woman, a human mother. As such her place in the "history of salvation" is unique and essential. It is from her that the unique Savior, Christ the God-man, received his full humanity. A woman, as Nicholas Cabasilas has written, "gave to him the whole of humanity." The unique vocation of Mary makes her inimitable. It is crucial to emphasize opposition to a rather pathetic, moralizing approach which would make of her a model for submissive women. Reflection upon the mystery of Mary can and does confirm women in the consciousness of their dignity as human persons. As God wanted to need Mary, so also has he need of women, her sisters. As he did with Mary, so also does he wish to do with women who are his free and responsible co-workers, according to the mysterious synergy of grace and human freedom, in the realization of his plan of love. They too can engage therefore with all of their being, heart, will, and intelligence in the total gift of self in faith which is the veritable glory of Mary. Like Mary, they respond to God's call, a singular appeal addressed to each and every one, a vocation to a destiny ordinary or extraordinary and filled with risks, as that of Mary. They too follow the example of Mary insofar as she is the figure of the true disciple, the model of the authentic following of Christ. As was the case with Mary, such is not confined to stereotypic roles. As with Mary, women can step courageously ahead in new and creative ways in their traditional vocations as spouses, mothers, and monastics, but in these nevertheless, always exploring, discerning the signs of the times, the new paths to which God has called them.

The little group around the cross, Mary, the women, and the disciple whom Jesus loved, represent the Church as the Lord wished the Church to be: a community of disciples, equal, one in faith, in hope beyond all human hopes, one in the "love strong as death," a vision quite the opposite of all too hierarchical arrangements but also opposed to the "women's church" to which some feminist theologians aspire.

A woman, a human being, called to participate in a unique way in accomplishing God's plan for humanity, Mary, according to the fundamental Tradition of the Church, is not an archetype of "woman" or of feminine holiness. She is rather a figure of the Church, of the body of Christ, of which men and women both are members, all of them called, as St Ambrose said, to become "mothers of Christ," to bring to birth in each and every person, in themselves and in the world, the complete Christ, *totus Christus*. On the symbolic level, Mary is the anticipation of the new man, the new being and new humanity, transfigured. In G. K. Chesterton's expression, quoted by Bishop Kallistos Ware, "Men are men, but Man is a woman."[26]

That integral humanity bears in Mary the characteristics of a woman; such symbolism contains deep meaning. In identifying with Mary, all of us Christian men and women are called in our relationship to God to an attitude of receptivity, of openness to the other and to the sacrifice of which, according to the ancient symbolism of the Bible, the bridegroom and the beloved are the figures.

Does this symbolism imply different ministries in the historical Church for men and for women? With some other Orthodox theologians, I think that this question remains open.

NOTES

1. *Le Ministère de la femme dans l'Eglise* (Paris: Cerf, 1987). However, the title of the English version is *The Ministry of Women in the Church* (Torrance, CA: Oakwood, 1991).

2. Such is the thesis, for example, of the Franco-Russian theologian Paul Evdokimov whose important work, *Woman and the Salvation of the World* (trans. Anthony P. Gythiel; Crestwood, NY: St Vladimir's Seminary Press, 1994), translated into a number of languages, has been widely read.

3. Olivier Clément, *L'Oeil de feu* (Fata Morgana), p. 18.

4. Tertullian, *On the dress of women*.

5. *The Sacrament of Love*, trans. Anthony P. Gythiel and Victoria Steadman (Crestwood, NY: St Vladimir's Seminary Press, 1985), pp. 17-18. This assimilation of Eve's guilt by women in Byzantine hymnography is the subject of the investigation of the American Byzantinologist Eva Topping, "Eve humiliée," *Contacts*, no. 156, 1991:4.

6. Olivier Clément, *Questions sur l'homme* (Paris: 1975), pp. 114-115.

7. See Maria Antonietta Macciocchi, ed., *Le donne secondo Wojtyla* (Milan: 1992). This volume is a collection of the reactions of a certain number of women theologians, mine also, to the letter *Mulieris Dignitatem*.

8. *Mulieris Dignitatem*, Editions Mediaspaul, p. 15.

9. Ibid., pp. 46-47.

10. Ibid., p. 16.

11. Ibid., p. 5.

12. Ibid., pp. 98-99.

13. Ibid., p. 111.

14. Paul Evdokimov, *op. cit.*, ch. 3.

15. Ibid., p. 216.

16. Ibid., p. 219.

17. Ibid., p. 259.

18. "On the Male Character of the Priesthood," in *Women and the Priesthood*, ed. Thomas Hopko (Crestwood, NY: St Vladimir's Seminary Press, 1983). [Trans. note: The second edition has just been published (1999), with new essays by all the surviving contributors, Bishop Kallistos Ware and Fr Hopko included.]

19. See the special issue of the journal *Contacts* devoted to this conference, no. 146, 1989:2.

20. Ibid., p. 96.

21. See Elisabeth Behr-Sigel, "L'Ordination des femmes, un problème oecuménique," *Contacts* no. 150, 1990:2; also "L'Ordination des femmes: une question posée aussi aux églises orthodoxes," in *Communion et Réunion* (Leuven: 1995).

22. *De ambiguiis*, pp. 1308-1309.

23. Nicholas Cabasilas, "Homélies mariales," in *Patrologie orientale* XIX, ed. M. Jugie (Paris: 1925).

24. Lev Gillet, "Marie, mère de Jesus," *Contacts*, no. 108, 1979:2, p. 374.

25. Unlike the Catholic Church, the Orthodox churches have made no dogma out of what is so powerfully suggested by the poetry of the liturgy.

26. Kallistos Ware, "Man, Woman, and the Priesthood of Christ," in *Women and the Priesthood*, p. 21.

10

Women in the Orthodox Church[*]

"Oh, strange Orthodox Church... Church of contrasts: at the same time so traditional yet so free, so ritualistic... yet so alive. Church where the gem of a prize, the Gospel, is preciously preserved, sometimes under a layer of dust... but who knows how to sing like no other the joy of Easter."

— Fr Lev Gillet

Of these contrasts recalled by a great spiritual Orthodox contemporary, Archimandrite Lev Gillet, the status of Orthodox women provides a particularly astonishing example. Here are juxtaposed and joined the liberating message of the Gospel and archaic taboos, a theological anthropology both spiritual and personal and the misogynistic stereotypes inherited from patriarchal societies. A femininity both serious and tender radiates from the omnipresent icons of the Mother of God, but access to the altar is forbidden to women. First to announce the resurrection of Christ, the myrrhbearing women of Easter morning are honored in the Orthodox churches with the title "Apostles to the Apostles." However, the reading of the Gospel during public worship remains reserved for male ministers. The list goes on and on. Beneath the shell of opaque customs and rituals nevertheless run spring-like waters. In different forms, today as in times past, women are participating in the life of the Orthodox Church. In contact with the modern world, an awareness takes shape. The call to the discernment of the position of women, found somewhere between the living Tradition and rigid traditionalism, is a "sign of the times." Will it be discerned? Will it be followed?

The common vocation of all the baptized, both women and men, is proclaimed prophetically in the sacraments of Christian initiation. They are given to all in the Orthodox Church, without gender distinction, through a

---

* Originally published in *The St Nina Quarterly*, vol. 2, no. 2, Spring 1998, and translated by Deno Takles.

profound and symbolic ritual. Baptism by immersion signifies a passage, a birth into the new life in communion with the death and the resurrection of Christ. Chrismation, the affixing of the seal of the Holy Spirit on different parts of the body, makes each person one of the Lord's anointed. As explained by Fr Lev Gillet, through baptism we become another Christ, joined through the Spirit with the Anointed One, Jesus Christ.[1] As the choir sings, "As many as have been baptized into Christ, have put on Christ,"[2] the newly baptized female (just as the newly baptized male), dressed in her baptismal gown, is introduced to the eucharistic assembly, the visible body of Christ of which she has become a member. However, at the same time that all separation appears to be abolished by virtue of our baptism, a ritual usually follows that seems to contradict that notion. The baptized male is led into the sanctuary behind the iconostasis, while its doors remain closed for the woman or the girl. Today, a growing number of Orthodox women feel that this ritual is discriminatory and wish for it to change.

What is the teaching concerning women of those called the Fathers of the Church, whose authority is great in the Orthodox Church?

The accusation of misogyny comes, above all, from the western feminists referring to the Latin traditions from Augustine to Thomas Aquinas and Bonaventure. Some Orthodox voices have joined this choir, like those of the Greek-American Byzantine hymnography specialist Eva Catafygiotou-Topping[3] and the Romanian theologian Anka Manalache.[4] Verna Nonna Harrison provides an in-depth study of gender themes in the anthropology of the Greek Fathers in her article, "Femininity and Masculinity in the Theology of the Cappadocian Fathers."[5] Veritable founders of Orthodox theological anthropology, the Cappadocian Fathers—Basil of Caesarea, Gregory of Nyssa, and Gregory of Nazianzus, and after them Maximus the Confessor—vigorously affirm the ontological unity within the distinction of persons in the humanity of man and of woman. This is according to the order of creation, an order distorted by the sin that is essentially separation, but restored in Christ according to the order of redemption. Genesis 1:27-28 and Galatians 3:27-28 are found at the heart of their anthropological meditation. "The woman possesses, just as the man does, the privilege of having been created in the image of God. Both their natures are equally honorable," is Basil's reply to the woman whose own doubts have led her to question him on this topic.[6] In his commentary on the baptismal hymn from the epistle to the Galatians, Basil evokes the image of Christ who is present in all who are baptized. Baptism eclipses the differences of race, social status, and gender: "Like in the portrait of the emperor, the beauty of the face transfigures the material used by the artist, be it wood or gold, rendering it without importance."[7] Summarizing the theological anthropology of the Cappadocian Fathers, Gregory of Nazianzus proclaims, "The same creator for man and for woman, for both the same clay, the same image, the same death, the same resurrection."[8]

Behind this discourse are the images of the real women who inspired it: the martyr Julitta whose example Basil urges Christian men and women to follow;[9] Macrina the Elder, confessor of the faith, and grandmother of Basil the Great and Gregory of Nyssa; Nonna, mother of Gregory of Nazianzus, who brought her husband to the Orthodox faith; and Gorgonia, her sister, described as a woman instructed in Scripture, assiduous in prayer, and generous to the poor. The most significant figure representing the condition of Christian women in the Cappadocian milieu is Macrina the Younger,[10] the elder sister of Basil the Great and Gregory of Nyssa. Her brothers speak about her as if she were their teacher. Gregory composed the *Dialogue on the Soul and the Resurrection*, a dialogue which he had with his dying sister, a text compared to Plato's *Phaedo*.

For the Fathers, woman, far from being just a sexual object, is the "opposite," the "other," with whom they must dialogue; their companion, at times their teacher, in spiritual combat. Their egalitarianism is situated in the eschatological perspective of the completeness of the end of time when genital sexuality will be transcended. Monasticism anticipates this completeness. It is in this context of an alternative society that the fundamental equality of women and men proclaimed in their anthropology is realized, not exclusively, but the most easily.

It is important to add that the patristic age coincides with the development of the female diaconate: a ministry directed to the service of women, corresponding to their precise needs in the heart of a patriarchal society. At the same time it is theologically founded, complete, liturgical, catechetical, philanthropic, and conferred by a veritable ordination, as is shown in the investigations of Professor Evangelos Theodorou.[11]

Still relatively unknown, the feminine face of Eastern Christianity remains open to further exploration. One knows little about the lives of Christian women during the dark centuries following the Hellenistic age up to the time of the splendor of Byzantium.

In the patriarchal agricultural societies which (at the end of the missionary expansion of Byzantine Christianity, and above all after the fall of Byzantium, around the Mediterranean and in the eastern part of Europe) became the terrestrial home of Orthodoxy, the luminous anthropology of the Gospel and of the Fathers lives in the depths of the ecclesial conscience. But, similar to the "hidden treasure in a field" of the Gospel parables, it finds itself buried under the slag of ancient taboos: the idea of the periodic ritual impurity of women taken from a misogynistic reading of Leviticus and truisms concerning women's weakness and inferiority. Nevertheless, the evangelical seed never stopped bearing fruit. The flame of feminine holiness has never been extinguished. The Church has canonized new martyrs, great monastics, and princesses like Olga of Kiev, venerated with her grandson Vladimir as "Equal to the Apostles." She has also canonized ordinary laywomen like Juliana Lazarevskaya in Russia, who lived at the dawn of modern time, whose "Life," composed by her own son, exalts her heroic charity.[12]

Closer to us, there are the images of the "women believers"—simple peasants and aristocrats, virtuous women and prostitutes—in the great Russian literature of the nineteenth century: the princess Maria of *War and Peace*, Sonia in *Crime and Punishment*, and the pathetic mothers looking for consolation with the *starets* Zosima in *The Brothers Karamazov*.

What about today? What is the position of women in the heart of an Orthodox Church that in the twentieth century has ceased to be monolithically "eastern," both geographically and culturally? Diverse emigrations have established (and inculturated) Orthodox communities in western Europe, America, and as far as Australia. Western modernity invades traditionally Orthodox countries: Greece, Romania, and Russia. In what ways has this marriage of different cultures modified the life and the status of the Orthodox Christian? I will limit myself to a few comments, as an exhaustive response would go beyond the scope of this article.

During the recent, and often dramatic, history of the Orthodox churches, women have assumed important responsibilities. It was notably the case in Russia under the Soviet regime. It is very well known that it was women—often older women, the well-known *babushki* or grandmothers—who saved the parish structures of the Russian Orthodox Church from total destruction by the atheistic state. Grandmothers had their grandchildren secretly baptized. They also put themselves up as volunteers to be part of the "twenty," the group of women believers, according to the legislation instituted under Khrushchev, to whose demands for a place of worship the state would concede. It was frequently also a woman who accepted the title and responsibility of *starosta* (a layperson responsible for the day to day running of the parish), as well as serving as intermediary or buffer between the civil authorities and the priest whom she strove to protect from their harassment. The survival of a parish depended on the tenacity and cleverness of these old women.

At the same time, other Christian Russian women found themselves among those named as dissidents: editors of *samizdats* and organizers of clandestine religious seminars, they were condemned to the heavy punishments of prison and the Gulag. What happened to them? One no longer hears too much about them.

Of the Christian women dissidents in the USSR, one can pick out an Orthodox nun who exercised her ministry—a "diaconal" ministry, writes her biographer—in the heart of the Russian emigration in France, first in the period between the wars, then under the German occupation. A former socialist revolutionary who returned to the Church, a friend of the great Russian religious thinkers (including Sergius Bulgakov and Nikolai Berdiaev), Mother Maria Skobtsova is one of the emblematic figures, like the pastor Dietrich Bonhoeffer, of the Christian resistance to the Nazi barbarians. Deported to the camp in Ravensbrück for having organized a network of escape for the Jews in Paris, she died there, possibly in the gas chamber, on the eve of Easter in 1945. Her canonization by the Orthodox Church is currently in progress.[13]

Today, after the fall of communism, some younger women—often neophytes—have taken over for the "grandmothers" of the Soviet era. Often enough, endowed with a good university education, these new Christian women fly to the aid of overworked priests, filling in as social assistants, but also as economists, accountants, architects, altogether animating the rebirth of parish life. It is women who assume the essential ministry of the Church to victims of brutal and chaotic economic changes: senior citizens, the homeless, children, large families, and the handicapped.

Among these deaconesses without the title, do some of them aspire to recognition by the Church by means of a blessing, or even a genuine ordination of their ministry? This aspiration does exist here and there. One finds it mostly among cultivated women who have a theological education. This aspiration has old roots in Russia. A restoration project of the ancient order of deaconess, an order fallen into disuse but never officially abolished in the Orthodox Church, was launched in the middle of the nineteenth century—possibly under Protestant influence—by women of the high aristocracy. They were encouraged by some enlightened bishops like the famous Metropolitan Philaret (Drozdov) of Moscow. Revisited at the beginning of the twentieth century by the Grand Duchess Elizabeth, it could not succeed during the dramatic circumstances of the time. Assassinated at the beginning of the Bolshevik revolution, Elizabeth Feodorovna was recently canonized. But her audacious project lies dormant in the archives of the patriarchate of Moscow. In the Russian Church (on which now blows the wind of fundamentalism mixed with an anti-western sentiment), at the end of a long period of glaciation, it is not the order of the day. Only a small minority of women know about it and are interested in it. For many reasons which would be interesting to analyze, feminism as developed in the West remains altogether strange to Christian Russian women. They maintain that they do not need it. The principle of obeying a spiritual father who is a priest or a monk (and there are also spiritual mothers!), inherited from monastic spirituality, far from being contested finds fervent followers among the newly converted women. Paradoxically, these "submissive" women often represent, in the heart of the new parishes and fraternities as they are created in Russia, the most dynamic and even dominating element, at the same time moved by an immense devotion. The Church, like Russian society, notes Veronica Lossky who knows them well, "is antinomically at the same time patriarchal and matriarchal."[14]

In addition, in eastern Europe and in the Middle East where Orthodoxy constitutes the traditional form of Christianity, and in the *diaspora* where during the twentieth century, Orthodox communities were formed and inculturated in the West, Orthodox women today continue to take an active role in the life of the Church. Their role for the transmission of the faith in the heart of the family, as much as mothers and educators, was always essential. But today it largely extends beyond this familial framework. Women, either alone or in equal partnership with male catechists, work in religious education. They sing in the choir, a role so important in Orthodox worship, and sometimes they even direct it. They are members (at least in the Church which originated with the Russian emigration) of the parish and diocesan councils like the diocesan assembly which elects the bishop. They participate in various aspects of community life. An important step was taken when, during the second half of the twentieth century, women were admitted as students to the schools of theology in different local Orthodox churches, notably in Greece and in the *diaspora* in France and the United States. Now they are beginning to teach in these schools of theology. Women as Orthodox theologians participate in ecumenical dialogues at all levels, notably at the heart of the ecumenical World Council of Churches. This has led to an enlightening paradox: an Orthodox Christian woman who has the training and the competence could teach the New Testament in a prestigious theology department like that of Thessalonika, but she would not be able to read the Gospel in the assembly of the people of God. An Orthodox theological conference unanimously proclaimed that "all acts denying the dignity of the human person, all discrimination between men and women based on gender is a sin,"[15] but access to the altar remains forbidden to women.

Today the question concerning the access of women to the sacramental ministry is addressed to the Orthodox Church more from the outside, in the context of ecumenical dialogues. But it has also become an internal problem for serious theologians, men and women, in light of the contradictions posed by the changing roles of women in the Church.[16] From the first international conferences of Orthodox women at the Monastery of Agapia in Romania (1976), and later at the Orthodox Academy of Crete (1989), the issue of the ordination of women was to be examined seriously and calmly. At the Interorthodox Consultation of Rhodes (1988) on the "ordination of women and the place of women in the Church," a consultation convoked and organized by the Ecumenical Patriarchate, the decision to restore the diaconate for women was unanimously adopted. More recently, this same wish was energetically revisited by the Orthodox Christian women who met at Damascus (October 1996) and in Istanbul (May 1997) for conferences organized according to the Gospel saying "interpret the signs of the times" (Mt 16:3).

The ordination of women to the priesthood remains unacceptable to most Orthodox for reasons having to do with liturgical symbolism. But does the ordination of women to the priesthood constitute a genuine heresy, a rupture with the teachings of Christ? The first Orthodox theologians confronted with this question were not prepared to answer but were forced to think about it. Today the search for the answers to these questions are more nuanced, and at the same time more rigorous.

"One of the most basic problems facing theologians today is knowing how to discern between the holy Tradition of the Church—the expression adequate or appropriate to Revelation—and the human traditions which express Revelation only imperfectly and, very often, which even oppose and obscure it,"[17] wrote Fr John Meyendorff of blessed memory in a book published thirty-five years ago but still current and recently re-edited. We are growing in numbers, men and women Orthodox theologians who call for an end to certain "traditional" practices of our historical churches regarding women; as stated in the conclusions of the Consultation of Rhodes, "owing to human weakness and sinfulness, Christian communities have not always and in all places been able to suppress effectively ideas, manners, and customs, historical developments and social conditions, which have resulted in practical discrimination against women."[18]

Finally, it is the supreme will of God that the Church become what she is: a community in faith, hope, and love, of men and of women, of the mystery of individuals, ineffably equal yet different, in the image and radiance of the divine Trinity. Such is the grand ecclesiological vision of the Orthodox Church. What remains is to translate it into our historical, empirical existence: a difficult task, seemingly impossible, to which we sometimes feel called, confident in the promise of the Christ to send us the Spirit from above who "will introduce the disciples to the entire Truth" (Jn 16:13).

NOTES

1. Lev Gillet, *Orthodox Spirituality* (Crestwood, NY: St Vladimir's Seminary Press, 1978), pp. 64-65.

2. Galatians 3:27.

3. Eva Catafygiotou-Topping, *Holy Mothers of Orthodoxy* (Minneapolis: Light and Life Publishing, 1987).

4. Anka Manalache, "Orthodoxy and Women," in *Women, Religion, and Sexuality*, ed. Jeanne Becher (Geneva: WCC, 1991).

5. Verna Nonna Harrison, "Male and Female in Cappadocian Theology," *Journal of Theological Studies*, 1990:8. See also *Contacts*, no. 179, 1997:2.

6. *On the Origin of Man*, Homily 1:18.

7. *Treatise on Baptism*, cited by Harrison.

8. Discourse 37:6.

9. In his eulogy of her, Basil puts in her mouth an exegesis of Genesis 2:21-22 that today would qualify as feminist.

10. Concerning Macrina the Younger, see Ruth Albrecht, *Das Leben der Heiligen Makrina auf dem Hintergrund der Thekla-Traditionen* (Göttingen, 1986).

11. Evangelos Theodorou, "L'Institution des diaconesses dans l'église orthodoxe," *Contacts*, no. 146, 1989:2. (Ed. note: See Kyriaki Karidoyanes Fitzgerald, *Women Deacons in the Orthodox Church: Called to Holiness and Ministry*, [Boston: Holy Cross, 1998].)

12. Elisabeth Behr-Sigel, *Prière et sainteté dans l'Eglise russe* (Begrosses: Bellefontaine, 1950), pp. 109-113.

13. Véronique Lossky, "La Femme et le sacerdoce," *Contacts*, no. 174, 1996:2.

14. Véronique Lossky, "La place de la femme dans l'Eglise orthodoxe et la question de l'ordination des femmes," *Contacts*, no. 146, 1989:2, p. 102.

15. "The Place of the Woman in the Orthodox Church and the Question of the Ordination of Women" (Istanbul: The Ecumenical Patriarchate, 1988); *Contacts*, no. 146, 1989:2, p. 102.

16. For more on this issue see my articles, "L'ordination des femmes; une question posée aussi aux Eglises orthodoxes," and "L'ordination des femmes: un problème oecuménique," *Contacts*, no. 150, 1990:2. English translations in *Sobornost*, 13:1 1991 and *Theology*, 1994:2 (SPCK).

17. John Meyendorff, *The Orthodox Church* (Crestwood, NY: St Vladimir's Seminary Press, 1996), p. x.

18. *Contacts*, no. 146, 1989:2, p. 102.

Nearly a Century of Life

by Lyn Breck

Once you have read the many writings of Elisabeth Behr-Sigel—her books, her articles, her conference presentations, her letters, her regular contributions to her local parish journal—you will want to meet her. You will want to know how, over nearly a century, God has inspired her works, her life, her actions, her decisions. How has divine grace entered and sustained her life? In the immense tapestry of the Church and its witness in the world, how has this one woman's presence made a difference? Elisabeth's natural curiosity, her gregariousness, and her understanding of Church as a place of communion have allowed her to form deep and lasting bonds of fellowship with people of all ages and all walks of life. From a very young age, God's plan was unfolding in her; her life forms an intricate pattern of holy searching, scholarly integrity, and spiritual depth. God's mercy is evident in her personal struggles and in the communal difficulties she assumed with others as their sister and mother in Christ.

Her spiritual father for many years, Fr Lev Gillet, commonly known as the Monk of the Eastern Church, left her the legacy of this wise counsel: "We must live and assume the tensions and the heartbreaks in faith." His spiritual nurturing over a relationship of fifty years provided guidance, sustenance, and courage to Elisabeth as she put into practice this call to faith. This is the same man who told many of his spiritual children: "Do not plan your future life and activity, but simply surrender all to the will of God." The thread of surrender to God's will is visible in Elisabeth's life.

Beloved Strasbourg

July 21, 1907: On this day Elisabeth Sigel was born in the town of Schiltigheim, near Strasbourg, in Alsace-Lorraine. Strasbourg, a "beautiful and marvelous city" according to the old German song, was at one time a Roman outpost named Argentoratum, later a free town in the heart of the Holy Roman Empire during the Middle Ages. In the seventeenth century, it was one of the centers of the Protestant Reformation. In 1681, the town was joined to the Catholic kingdom of France under King Louis XIV. The Protestants were greatly displeased. A century later, the Protestant bourgeoisie of Strasbourg, to which Elisabeth's father's family belonged, rallied with enthusiasm behind the ideals of the French Revolution of 1789, proclaiming that all men were born free and equal. The revolutionary hymn "La Marseillaise," that later became the national anthem of France, was composed in Strasbourg. As such, Elisabeth's Alsacian ancestors came to consider themselves French, though Elisabeth herself grew up speaking both French and German.

Elisabeth's family had both Protestant and Jewish roots. Elisabeth's mother, Emma Altshul,

> was born into a Jewish family in Central Europe in the town of Ceskalipa, north of Bohemia. At the time, this region was part of the Austro-Hungarian Empire. Emma considered herself to be Austrian, though she spoke both German and Czech. The spiritual climate of the family was liberal Jewish. My maternal grandmother was Sophie Freud, who shared the family name of Sigmund Freud, founder of psychoanalysis, also an Austrian Jew from this same area. Emma's father was a merchant. Other family members were doctors. One of my mother's cousins, Greta Meisel-Hess, was a well-known avant garde writer. As a child, I would spend wonderful vacations in Bohemia with my grandmother. I was the 'little goy.' I was cherished by the Jewish side of my family. They were quite simply an integral part of Austrian society.

A large number of Elisabeth's family members were caught in the Nazi persecution during the Second World War and died in the concentration camps at Prague and Auschwitz. Elisabeth's mother was among those who escaped in time.

A painting of Strasbourg hangs over the desk in Elisabeth's study. As she spoke of her time in Strasbourg where she grew up and attended the university, her face softened. She smiled. The place of her birth has left a warm spot in her heart. She said of Strasbourg, "The town of my childhood was open and receptive." However, it was also a place where she experienced tragedy.

A Childhood Crisis

In 1918, at the end of the Great War, Strasbourg and all of Alsace-Lorraine, which had belonged to Germany since the end of the Franco-Prussian War in 1870, once again became a part of France. But German families were no longer allowed to live in Alsace-Lorraine. Elisabeth's best friend, Herta, was a young German girl. Her father, deeply troubled by the situation and finally in a state of a despair, committed suicide. Shocked by the tragedy, the two girls, both eleven years old, decided to attend Sunday services at the local Protestant church. They made the decision on their own without any influence from their elders. "My little friend and I went to church together as if for the first time," Elisabeth reported.

The personal experience of tragedy at the threshold of adolescence helped to solidify Elisabeth's religious understanding. Commenting on the event, Elisabeth said, "I knew I was a Protestant. When I was a year old, I was baptized by a Lutheran pastor, a friend of my father's who would send me a Christmas gift each year. The meaning of my baptism was never explained to me. My father, Charles Sigel, an Alsacian, went to the Protestant church once a year on Good Friday. I didn't go with him. My mother would shut herself up in her room on the Jewish holy day of Yom Kippur with a prayer book that I still have. However, she never went to the synagogue. Sometimes I went to the synagogue with my maternal grandmother. But at home, we never spoke about religion. In my private Protestant school, there was religious instruction. Jesus was presented as someone who gave out commandments that were beautiful but difficult to follow. For example, 'Love your enemies.' Now in a vague way, I was looking for a source of consolation. After my first Sunday at church, I asked my parents to sign me up for catechism classes so I could prepare for confirmation as a Protestant. It was my own choice to 'consciously choose the faith of the Church.'" Thereafter Elisabeth became a committed Christian. Her catechism classes were taught by a very kind man with extremely liberal ideas, and Elisabeth regularly challenged him with such questions as, "What is the communion of saints?"

After her confirmation, during which she was deeply touched, she decided to join a Protestant youth movement, "la FEDE," the French branch of "la FUACE" (the World Student Christian Federation). This happened just after World War I during which a whole generation of fathers and brothers had been decimated. Now a new Christian generation aspired to a great spiritual renewal that would somehow overcome the catastrophe of war. These same students who belonged to the Protestant Student Association gathered university students of all faiths under the slogan "that they all may be one" (John 17:1) to form a fledgling ecumenical movement long before the advent of institutional ecumenism. Later Elisabeth herself would affirm that a true ecumenical vocation requires an effort of understanding on two levels, that of theology and that of witness. In this context, Elisabeth met many great believers who strengthened her faith. In particular, there were Marc Boegner, a pastor who in 1948 became one of the founders of the World Council of Churches, and Suzanne de Dietrich, an organizer of the youth camps Elisabeth attended.

As her teen years came to a close, Elisabeth was struck by another tragedy as she watched her mother die of cancer. At the age of ninety-three, Elisabeth still mourns this loss: "I was too young to lose my mother." Her adolescence was marked by these two tragedies of untimely death.

The University Years

In spite of these experiences of loss, Elisabeth retained her enthusiasm for learning. In 1926, the Protestant Faculty of Theology of the University of Strasbourg made a radical decision: to admit women as regular students! "Enrolled as a philosophy student at the Faculty of Letters," Elisabeth commented, "I was among the first women to take advantage of this more open policy. Paradoxically, it was here at the Protestant university that I had my first contact with Orthodoxy. My friends included a group of young Russian Orthodox immigrants who had received special fellowships to study in Strasbourg. We were drawn together by our common interest in Christian unity. We discussed theology and ecclesiology.

"These same friends introduced me to the notion of sobornost," Elisabeth continued,

> the conciliarity of the Church, and with that to the great Russian lay theologian of the nineteenth century, Alexis Khomiakov. I was drawn to his way of thinking because he went beyond the Protestant-Catholic dichotomy in attempting to reconcile a spirit of freedom with faithfulness to tradition. On one occasion, when my Russian friends and I traveled to Paris to attend the Student Movement Council, they invited me to attend the Easter celebrations at St Sergius Orthodox Theological Institute chapel. The school had just been founded in 1925. At the age of 21, for the first time in my life, I attended an Or-

thodox Pascal Matins service. I was completely changed by the experience. I felt myself flooded with a light so bright that it turned away all darkness, all questions, all anxieties. I made a decision at that moment. I absolutely had to learn more about this ancient yet young Orthodox Church, heir of the united Church of the first centuries. I needed permission to continue my theological studies in Paris for at least a semester. During the 1920s, Paris was the capital of Russian immigration. With some difficulty, I was finally allowed to enroll in the Protestant Faculty of Theology in Paris on Boulevard Arago.

At about the same time, she was instrumental in founding within the "Fede" a special group for foreign student relations. Scholarships established at Strasbourg University for Russian Orthodox immigrants allowed many of them to be students of the theological department. Through this special student group for foreign students, Elisabeth made new friends. They invited her to attend Orthodox Easter at the Church of St Sergius in Paris where Father Sergius Bulgakov was the celebrant. That year, 1928, turned out to be an important one. At twenty-one years of age, she made the decision to pursue her interest in Orthodoxy and requested admission to the University of Paris. That same year, she met Fr Lev Gillet, an encounter that changed her life. At that time, the very first Orthodox parish where services were celebrated in French was forming.

Elisabeth shared how she managed during this time. "I would go to the Protestant Church on Boulevard de la Gare one Sunday and to the Orthodox Church the next Sunday while attending courses on Thomism with the Catholics." By the end of the next year, she had entered the Orthodox Church. Fr Lev Gillet came to Strasbourg where he celebrated the liturgy. The actual service of her entry to Orthodoxy took place in a student room which happened to be the room of Andre Behr, her future husband. Still, she said, "I owe my conversion to Protestantism. That is where I encountered Christ."

In their totality, Elisabeth's studies took place at three universities: Strasbourg, Paris, and one semester in Berlin. She received her "license," comparable to a Master's degree in philosophy, and her "maitrise" in theology, roughly a doctoral level degree. During these years as a student, she was greatly influenced by her personal contacts with Nikolai Berdiaev, Father Sergius Bulgakov, and Simeon L. Frank, all of whom had been expelled from Russia and served as a meeting-point between East and West. It was a time when she developed critical skills in reflection and refined her vocation as a teacher.

A Pastoral Ministry

Ville-Climont was a small rural mountain village inhabited essentially by farmers. This parish had been deprived of a pastor since the end of the First World War. Many of the men had not returned from the battlefields. Elisabeth had graduated first in her class at the university, so she was called in by the "ecclesiastical inspector" of the Reformed Church of Alsace-Lorraine and asked, "What shall we do?" He appointed though did not ordain her (the French expression is *délégation pastorale*) to preach and exercise a pastoral ministry when she was just twenty-four years old. By this time she had already converted to Orthodoxy, but she took the assignment anyway with the support and encouragement of Fr Sergius Bulgakov.

She generally rode up the hill on a bike to the village. In Ville-Climont, she led the prayers in church, taught religion to the children, visited people in their homes, and provided spiritual nourishment to the people of the area. They welcomed her. This was a joyful ministry for her. She recalled that "they used to bring me butter."

Her experience in Ville-Climont lasted almost one year. All the while she was engaged and planning to marry. At that time it was inconceivable that a married woman should assume a pastoral ministry. It was a sad parting. This experience, however, left Elisabeth Sigel with a yearning to realize her true ministry as a woman in the Church. It left her with hope. This woman theologian was a trailblazer, the first to have such a ministry in France.

Engagement and Marriage

As a young child in Russia, Andre Behr had witnessed the imprisonment of his father and his stepmother when he was ten. The Soviets had taken the family lands. Before that he had suffered the heartbreak of his parent's divorce. His mother died just before the Russian revolution. At the age of twelve, Andre came to France alone. He lived in Nice, where his stepmother had a villa, and attended a Catholic school there. He was able to integrate into French society. Soon he even hesitated to speak Russian.

Elisabeth and Andre met when they were both students. They traveled in some of the same circles and both were involved in the Russian Student Christian Movement (l'ACER), which had been started in 1923. They shared ecumenical interests as well. Their courtship took place over the time Elisabeth was exercising her pastoral ministry in Ville-Climont. They married in 1932 and lived in Nancy, where together they founded one of the first ecumenical reflection groups in France. Andre worked as an engineer in Lorraine. Elisabeth was hired to teach philosophy in the public school system. They had their first child, Nadine, in 1934. Shortly afterwards Marianne was born, in 1936.

During their early years as a couple they befriended lay theologian Vladimir Lossky and his wife, Elisabeth. Their common interest was to provide an Orthodox Christian witness in the West. Together they were a part of the first French language Orthodox parish, founded in 1929. Up to that time, all the other churches of the Russian immigration celebrated services in Slavonic. Elisabeth continued her research in the area of spirituality while giving attention to motherhood and family life. Her earliest works written at this time focused on the Russian idea of holiness and Sergius Bulgakov's theology.

The Shadow of War

Once again groanings, conflict, and discontent surfaced in Europe. Hitler was coming to power. A shadow was cast across western Europe. By the time war broke out in 1939, Nadine was five and Marianne was three. Fr Sergius Bulgakov was Elisabeth's spiritual father during the war. It was in large part because of Fr Sergius's encouragement that Elisabeth had assumed a kind of female diaconate several years earlier proclaiming the Gospel, teaching adults and children, and visiting the sick. Now she taught her own children.

At this time the resistance movement emerged in France. The ecumenical group founded on a common interest of faith now turned to social problems created by war. Nancy was in a restricted zone annexed by the Germans. People could no longer go about freely. The ecumenical group became the ecumenical resistance group; in Elisabeth's words, "We formed a group of spiritual resistance to Naziism." Several of its members were tortured and killed. In the outlying forests, resistance guerilla fighters hid out, waiting to strike the enemy. Elisabeth mentioned that "Olga and Alexis Mojaisky, our closest friends back then, encouraged us to protest, to help the Jews. The bonds of friendship we formed were profound and intense." Elisabeth and her husband offered assistance to many Jewish people during the war. They regularly took in Jewish children. Fr Lev would write false baptismal certificates for them. Mother Maria Skobtsova would hide them in her house at Rue Lourmel. This was a new form of diaconal ministry birthed in the crisis of war and persecution. Toward the end of the war, Elisabeth and Andre's third child, Nicholas, was born in Nancy during a bombing raid. This child was later baptized by Fr Elie Melia, a Georgian priest, who rode through the war zone on a bicycle to Belfort to perform the sacrament. Such were the times.

"During these years, I began to know the Jesus prayer," Elisabeth said. She wrote an article devoted to the Jesus prayer in 1947. It was intended as an introduction to hesychasm. "That same year Vladimir Lossky wrote his Mystical Theology of the Eastern Church," she continued. The publication of this book made it evident that the Orthodox Christian Church was not purely a Russian experience. A book written by Etienne Fouilloux, in French, *Catholics and Christian Unity in the Nineteenth and Twentieth Centuries*, has ten entries pertaining to the ecumenical group in Nancy and specifically to the role of Elisabeth Behr-Sigel. In 1947, Elisabeth became a member of the Fellowship of St Alban and St Sergius, an Anglican-Orthodox initiative inaugurated in 1927. Her ecumenical involvement expanded.

Another Challenge

Elisabeth still longed to pursue theological studies, but women were not allowed admission to the seminaries. In 1950, however, Leon Zander and Paul Evdokimov, theologians and professors at the St Sergius Institute, organized what were referred to as "free courses." They were held outside of St Sergius and were accessible to women. Elisabeth's friendship with Paul Evdokimov was very important in her life. "As a young woman," she said, "I was a nanny for Paul Evdokimov's children. I was asked to be the godmother of his son, Michel, who is now a priest and a theologian in his own right," she confided. Today they occasionally meet to share amicably their differing theological perspectives.

With Fr Lev's encouragement and support, Elisabeth gladly attended these free classes. She wrote "Prayer and Holiness in the Russian Church," which appeared in the journal Istina. But when their son Nicholas was still quite young, Andre became ill. Elisabeth returned to work, teaching philosophy in Verdun. Because of the commuting distance, she would stay the week in Verdun and return home on the weekends. Marianne would take care of her father and brother. "There was no other way," Elisabeth said matter-of-factly, "someone had to earn a living." Andre's illness was prolonged. He died in 1968 at the age of fifty-nine. By then Nicholas was fifteen years old and the girls were young women. Elisabeth still keeps a photo of Andre on her desk.

A Vocation Within a Vocation

Fr Lev Gillet's spiritual wisdom offered solace to Elisabeth in her time of bereavement. He had the great gift of listening and helped her to hold onto the kenotic vision of Christ who bears the suffering of the world. By now Elisabeth was collaborating on a regular basis with the Orthodox theological journal *Contacts* and was equally active in a variety of ecumenical publications such as *Irenikon*. By 1972, her theological search, which centered around the juxtaposition of the contemplation of the divine Logos and the incarnation, came to fruition in her work on Bukharev, *A Monk in the City*. In 1975, she obtained a doctorate from the University of Nancy upon completion of her studies at both Nancy and Paris. Subsequently she held several positions as professor at the St Sergius Institute in Paris, the Institute of Ecumenical Studies (associated with the Catholic Institute), the Ecumenical Institute of Tantur in Jerusalem, and the Dominican College of Ottawa, Canada. It is somewhat ironic that she became a professor at St Sergius, the very seminary that had earlier refused her admission because she was a woman.

A turning point in her life came when she received an invitation to present the opening address at the World Council of Churches gathering in Agapia, Romania. The theme of this conference was "The Community of Men and Women in the Church." She was sixty-nine years old at the time and still remembers the moment very well. "I was visiting Olivier Clément when I received the invitation. I was in such a state of shock that I literally sat down on the floor. I was the only French woman present in those meetings." It is important to note that this gathering took place in an ecumenical perspective.

Since this first meeting, Elisabeth has returned to pursue these dialogues which have focused more closely on the role of women in the Church. More recently she has raised the question of the ordination of women in the Orthodox Church. Refusing all polemical arguments, she encourages the Church to engage in a true theological reflection on this topic. "What kind of witness are we offering to young men and women if we refuse to dialogue?" she has asked. Her commitment to this topic crosses generational lines. At ninety-three years of age, she stresses her concern for the younger generation, their faith, and their place in the Church, and she challenges their elders in the faith not to close the doors on them nor on their questions.

Looking at the unfolding of Elisabeth's new vocation within a vocation, it is essential to remember that Elisabeth has never been a feminist at heart. She is simply a faithful Orthodox Christian woman legitimately concerned about the role of women in the Church. This is clear in her most recent publication, *L'Ordination des femmes dans l'Eglise orthodoxe* (*The Ordination of Women in the Orthodox Church*), published in cooperation with Bishop Kallistos Ware. She is also deeply concerned with bringing an end to torture; she was vice president of the Christian Association for the Abolition of Torture for ten years. She serves even now as a lay consultant to the Orthodox Interepiscopal Committee in France. A review of her writings provides a sense of her true vocation. In her church community, she has been given roles of leadership and a teaching ministry. Her theology and spirituality are grounded in a daily discipline of prayer. As she engages in theological and spiritual dialogue, she does so from an inspired faith and witness. There is no polemic, no animosity; rather, joy, integrity, and enthusiasm characterize her contributions.

Each Day Is a Day Fully Lived

This nearly one century of Elisabeth Behr-Sigel's life forms a splendid mosaic, colorful, beautiful, and profound. It is a gift to us. For it is not simply about one life. Instead, Elisabeth's life underscores the interconnections, the vast influences of small details and brief encounters of fellowship and commitment over time. The events of a lifetime find their place in the legacy of salvation history. She reminds us that we are the Church, the body of Christ. As members one of another, the Church saves us. We do not save the Church. Although this is a sketch of one woman's contribution throughout the twentieth century, it is absolutely clear that the whole story is not about one person making a solitary impression. And yet the faithfulness of one person in following God's calling, together with other faithful witnesses, form that vast cloud of witnesses which is the universal Church from generation to generation. Our response is gratitude to God for the gift he has bestowed to the whole Church through Elisabeth's life and witness.

Each day, Elisabeth awakes to a new joy, another task. Perhaps her activities will include telephone calls to family members, choosing some fruit and vegetables at the local market, or reviewing one of her latest presentations (as recently as December 1998) devoted to Orthodox theological formation in the twenty-first century. Perhaps she will prepare a meal for a guest, offering hospitality and solace, or she will greet a neighbor in the hallway, asking "How are you?" and really wanting to know. Many of us who know Elisabeth personally are impressed by her level of energy. Although we are much younger, we joke and lament that we cannot keep up with her. She has said herself, "I am never bored."

Others have said of her that she is an optimist with a profound spiritual conscience who has bestowed on the Church an enormous work of reflection. In her endeavors there is always an intentionality, a direction. Without words she challenges us to keep up with the evolution of God's plan for his people. Her life and work call us to continued exploration, an unrelenting search for spiritual truth and beauty to be lived out in all the details of daily life. She calls us to become open and vulnerable, to dare to hope, to engage in dialogue even when controversial. Her witness reminds us to trust God, to cast out into the deep, to take heart, to remember the holy accompaniment of the presence of Christ who is always with us, even unto the end of the age.

If there is one last image that is a vital part of Elisabeth Behr-Sigel's legacy to us, it is hope. This hope which she bears in her very way of being is birthed in love and self-sacrifice and nurtured in daily prayer and work, in communion with others, and is announced again and again in her theological writings. It is essentially an eschatological hope: "Thy kingdom come!" Maranatha...

Postscript

Elisabeth has had, over the course of this anthology project, many reservations about including her biography. She would suddenly say, "Wait until I'm no longer here," and then yet another adventure would catch her attention; another story from another time, yet all intimately connected in the present. I have tried to introduce the person I know, one who is full of life, whose eyes sparkle, whose genuine smile is heartwarming. She is a diminutive—less than five-foot-tall woman—who still climbs on chairs to reach almost everything in her kitchen as she prepares a meal. Despite her hesitations, there is the silent understanding that this story needs to be told not for purposes of self-aggrandizement but for God's glory. This is, in fact, the only acceptable way to put forth the intriguing narrative. Once upon a time, now, God was and is and ever shall be!

Epilogue
Orthodoxy, Modernity, and Feminism Recovered

by Sarah E. Hinlicky

O ne of the things that attracts people to Eastern Orthodoxy is the sheer ancientness of it. And since Orthodoxy claims to be the living embodiment of the undivided early Church, it takes ancientness seriously. The church fathers are still the premier theologians in the East, and the reign of the Byzantine empire lives on in the aesthetic vision of the Orthodox faithful, from the Near Eastern jurisdictions to the distant Siberian ones. Dim candle lighting and the smoke from incense evoke the memory of Christians from an era long past, either praying in the catacombs or flooding the basilicas, and their presence even now in the communion of saints is visibly attested by the company of icons all around.

This ancientness, along with the sense of the undivided Church, is precisely what attracted a young French woman named Elisabeth to the Orthodox Church in the early 1930s. Raised by a nominally religious Lutheran father and a lapsed Jewish mother, Elisabeth pursued her religious education on her own, from confirmation on through her adolescence. As a young adult she studied philosophy, which providentially prepared her to enter with the first class of women students in the Reformed Protestant theological faculty at the University of Strasbourg. Wary of the liberal inclinations of her professors and moved by the piety of her few Russian classmates, she began to explore the theological and ecclesiological dimensions of the Orthodox Church. After a complex spiritual evolution, as she calls it, Elisabeth converted to the Church where she had found "the foretaste of the beatitude that is the Kingdom of Heaven." But the great irony of Elisabeth's attraction and conversion to this very ancient Church is that, in joining it, she became an entirely new thing in it. Elisabeth Behr-Sigel is, one might say, the first lady of Orthodox women theologians.

Behr-Sigel is, indeed, uniquely qualified to earn that distinction. The circumstances of her life have placed her squarely at the crossroads both between East and West and between the ancient and modern worlds. She is, in the first place, a "Diaspora Orthodox"—of French origins, ecclesially allied with a Church that is the grandchild of the refugees of the Russian revolution, and located in a historically non-Orthodox nation. In this milieu she came to know personally all the great Orthodox thinkers of the twentieth century: Schmemann, Meyendorff, Berdiaev, Bulgakov, Evdokimov, and Gillet, allowing her even now to function as a living link to the Russian religious renaissance in western Europe. Her upbringing and university level training were Protestant, which taught her, as she has said, to draw on all the proper knowledge of the Enlightenment and a tradition that had had extensive traffic with the modern world as well as "a rich sense of Gospel freedom." And what is, in many ways, most important is the fact that Behr-Sigel is a woman. As the question—one might even say the "problem"—of women in the Church has moved closer and closer to the center of the Church's internal discussion, Behr-Sigel has found herself, a little unwillingly at first, blazing the trail for her Church to follow. In continuity with the aspirations of her nineteenth-century spiritual predecessors and her twentieth-century colleagues, her life project has been to bring the Church of the ancient world into honest contact with the modern world. Thus it is with good reason that she has been nicknamed "the grandmother of western Orthodoxy."

II

In the first place, the Orthodox conversation with modernity has required the basic recognition of earthly change. There is an unresolved tension between the eternal truth guarded by the Church and the relentless march of time. Orthodoxy still lags behind its western companions in confronting the problems and advances of modernity head-on, in part simply because the geographic East has lagged behind the West technologically. Although the Orthodox world positively overflows with a wealth of spiritual theology and devotional works, the failure to account for the enormous changes of the past several hundred years has had a detrimental effect on the health of the Eastern Church, as the recent book-burning in Russia aptly demonstrates. Coupled with the urgent need for recovery after the shipwreck of Communism and the redundancy of overlapping jurisdictions divided by ethnic claims, Orthodoxy has its work cut out for it. And that is exactly where Behr-Sigel comes in. From the inside, she has been able to take an honest look at the state of her ancient Church and admit, quite frankly, that while it must hold on to its ancient heritage, Orthodoxy needs modernity nonetheless.

The need begins on the wide social and national level. By way of sheer historical accident, the traditionally Orthodox countries, specifically the Slavic and Near Eastern ones, have nearly escaped the encounter with the Enlightenment altogether. At a time when western Europe and North America are struggling under the secular state's hushing of the voice of religion, these lands are still holding up the model of Church as midwife to the independent nation. For most of them, and most especially for Russia, the only exposure to modern statehood so far has been in the guise of oppressive Communist totalitarianism. Given the economic havoc wrought by the aggressive and senseless industrialization of Communist regimes, it is hardly surprising that the Orthodox countries are tempted to look backwards toward feudalism, monarchies, and struggles for ethnic sovereignty. Such is the misunderstood world of the Balkans.

Although the East never saw the kind of wars of religion provoked by the Reformation that killed so much of the spirit of western Europe, it has still been plagued by what the Orthodox Church itself has officially condemned as phyletism—literally, love of the tribe. Orthodoxy has always thrived, theologically speaking, on its conciliar model, with the Ecumenical Patriarch of Constantinople functioning solely as a "first among equals." But while the international Orthodox Church has never suffered from the theological controversies and schisms that have rocked the West, politically its uncentralized conciliarity has proved, at times, to be disastrous. The autocephalous churches, providing the essential cradle for nationhood, have also cultivated rivalries, even with other Orthodox nations, when unity would have spared these territories a great deal of political misery. It is imperative, notes Behr-Sigel, that the various cultural orthodoxies regain their sense of united Orthodoxy, by relinquishing the jurisdictional disputes and drawing again on the liturgical heritage common to all the Orthodox churches. Unity is all the more imperative as the world shrinks and the long-enclosed Orthodox territories are being exposed both to positive western values like democracy, tolerance, and human rights, as well as to the more pernicious western influences of consumerism, secularism, and rampaging fundamentalist missionaries. Behr-Sigel has repeatedly called upon the Orthodox Church to face up to the challenges of modernity before a backlash of either the reactionary or postmodern form strikes at the heart of the Church.

In-house resolution is not enough for Behr-Sigel, though. She believes that ecumenism is one of the brightest hallmarks of modernity. She has herself pursued avenues of ecumenical reconciliation, especially through her studies and teaching at various ecumenical institutes as well as the Roman Catholic faculty in Paris. It may come as a surprise that the World Council of Churches has been one of the greatest servants to the Orthodox world's fledgling ecumenical efforts and to Behr-Sigel's own work in it. The WCC, at one time, did much to bring Orthodox from all over the world together as well as provide opportunities for dialogue with other communions. A WCC-sponsored conference of Orthodox women in 1976 started Behr-Sigel on her groundbreaking reflections on women in Orthodox theology. (It is all the more regrettable, then, that the WCC now seems determined to self-destruct, or at least to evict de facto the Orthodox churches.) Ecumenical exchange has so far been a beneficial and revitalizing force for Orthodoxy, especially in the theologians of the Diaspora such as Schmemann and Meyendorff, and has even resulted in some unexpected discoveries—a new-found appreciation of Thomas Aquinas in the East, for example. Behr-Sigel speaks of "an Orthodoxy becoming conscious once again, but in the pain of its birthing, of its universal vocation." For now, however, the vocation falls short of universality. She openly acknowledges that only in the dialogue and, God willing, eventual reunion with the ostracized churches of the West can Orthodoxy fully attain to its own calling.

Continuing in her efforts to bring the ancient tradition into conversation with the contemporary situation, Behr-Sigel, though a wife and mother herself, has taken a keen interest in the role of monasticism for this modern world. She explores its significance specifically in two short biographies of monastics, revolutionaries in their own right, who turned their respective worlds upside down by facing modernity with all the strength of tradition behind them rather than hiding from its terrifying force. The first of these is Archimandrite Feodor (Alexander in the world) Bukharev, whose work and life story were absolutely formative in Behr-Sigel's own lifelong project. Bukharev emerged as the first of the Russian Orthodox to recognize the need for an encounter with modernity, his book *Orthodoxy and the World* calling for radical openness to culture and society based on the incarnation of God in man. Such a theological move earned him only the disdain of his seniors and the loss of his teaching position. As a result, Bukharev, recognizing the dishonesty by which he was led into the monastic life (at the time, the most promising young men were plucked early on to form a special "caste" of theology professors, monastic superiors, and bishops) and forced into practical exile for his writings, was laicized voluntarily, a thing almost unheard-of in the mid-nineteenth century. Yet even in his regained lay status, Bukharev found no essential difference in his Christian calling than he had had as a monk: as a married man, father, and theologian, he still lived according to the rule of poverty, chastity, and obedience. His twin considerations of the movement of the Logos through modern culture and the spiritual connection between the married and monastic life were extremely influential on the thinkers of the Russian religious renaissance in the West, Behr-Sigel and Evdokimov in particular.

Behr-Sigel's interest in monasticism emerges again in her short biography of Mother Maria Skobtsova. Mother Maria was a most unlikely candidate for sainthood—a revolutionary, a part of the turn-of-the-century Russian intelligentsia, and twice divorced. But upon finding herself a refugee among countless other displaced Russians in the first half of this century, she made her monastic profession and lived out the rest of her life a nun comparable to Dorothy Day, her passionate love for the Church spilling over into passionate love for the poor and social reform. Her conception of her vocation was intensely sacrificial, and far removed from the sterile models she found present in her Church at the time. In her article, Behr-Sigel highlights Mother Maria's vision to replace the old forms with new ones: "This [current] notion of monasticism, she thought, could possibly be appropriate at other times in our history. But this was an apocalyptic time, when we sensed the end of the world at hand. We must not forget that her concept of monasticism was developed in the 30s when fascism was at its height, the rise of the 'vile beast.' But it goes much further than that. Under the influence of Fr Lev Gillet, Mother Maria dreamt of a creatively renewed monasticism that would be a response to the vocation discerned in the 'signs of the times': monasticism not lived out behind protective walls but 'in the world.'" Her zeal for reform was not aimed against cloisters or contemplative orders in their own right, but rather the notion that there was only one (that is, cloistered and contemplative) expression of the monastic life. Her living out the Gospel in the world exacted its toll: Mother Maria lost her life in the concentration camps in Ravensbrück just days before the liberation.

The key phrase in Behr-Sigel's account of Mother Maria's monastic vision is "the signs of the times." Those several words taken from Jesus' charge to his disciples summarize Behr-Sigel's entire project of bringing Orthodoxy into encounter with modernity. Already evident is her commitment to the universalization of Orthodoxy, the ecumenical imperative, and the reinvention of monasticism. Dearest of all to Behr-Sigel's heart, though, is what she calls, in pointed contrast to feminism, the women's movement.

The Orthodox Church's attitude toward women is a study in remarkable contrasts. On the one hand there is a decided veneration, even idealization, of woman. The omnipresent icons of the Theotokos capture a femininity "both serious and tender," as Behr-Sigel describes it, respecting the highest honor accorded to a human being in Mary's motherhood to the Savior. The myrrh-bearing women who found the empty tomb and were the first witnesses to the resurrection are called the Apostles to the Apostles, Mary Magdalene even earning the title "Equal to the Apostles." Behr-Sigel indicates that the Church Fathers, still the primary authorities in the East, upheld the scriptural tradition of woman's high spiritual calling and capacity, even amidst the more frequently cited anti-woman remarks (such as Tertullian's "Woman is the gate to hell"). Patristic anthropology posits ontological equality between men and women, notes Behr-Sigel in her studies on the fathers, formulated in such expressions as "what is not assumed is not saved" (Athanasius) and "the same creator for man and for woman, for both the same clay, the same image, the same death, the same resurrection" (Gregory of Nazianzus). Likewise the assurance of Basil of Caesarea to a woman concerned about her standing before God: "The wife also, like the husband, has the privilege of being created in the image of God. Their two natures are equally honorable; equal are their virtues; equal are their rewards; and alike are their condemnations." In this light it is not at all surprising that a female diaconate flourished in the patristic period; even after it fell into disuse, women both married and celibate functioned as deaconesses without the name in Eastern communities, all the way down to the Soviet era.

So the vocation of women is respected and encouraged. Behr-Sigel comments, though, that idealization and subordination often go hand in hand. There still remains the strange residue of pre-Christian fears, unexamined stereotypes, and instances of low-level misogyny that sound to westerners like more of the unsubstantiated complaints of radical academic feminism. In reality, since the Orthodox world has been largely untouched by modernity, so has it eluded the purging of anti-woman sentiments. Behr-Sigel observes that while icons of the Mother of God decorate the altar, flesh and blood women are denied access to it themselves—except, that is, to clean it. By tradition (though not by canon) the latter-day sisters of the Apostles to the Apostles are not permitted to read aloud the words of the Scriptures during worship. Taboos of ritual impurity, both the monthly and postpartum kinds, are still observed in some places, although they are less likely to be practiced in the Diaspora communities—the ones whose people live daily in the modern world. There has been much controversy of late over "ordination" to the female diaconate, although the evidence accumulated thus far indicates that there was at one time such a liturgical rite and ecclesial status for women. Only in the latter part of this century have Orthodox women been admitted into theological studies at the university level, and in some places not even now. The question of women in the priesthood has even become an intra-Orthodox concern, as ecumenical dialogues, particularly with the Anglican Church, have brought it to the forefront. Just in the past decade has this matter been "internalized," at the prompting of Metropolitan Anthony Bloom in Great Britain, and several volumes of study by Orthodox theologians on the possibility of women in the priesthood been published, again with Behr-Sigel leading the way.

As such Behr-Sigel finds herself, like Abraham's wife Sarah, she says, at the ripe old age of ninety-three and yet expected to produce new life in her community, plotting a path for the Orthodox encounter with modernity to follow. Regarding the re-examination of church teaching on women, she has outlined the next three steps for Orthodox theology and practice to take. First, she insists that all canons referring to the ritual impurity of women be once and for all abolished, following the lead of the Messiah who associated with prostitutes and permitted a woman with an issue of blood to touch him. Second, she expects that Orthodox anthropology, grounded in the Fathers, can be explored and expounded to produce a humane model for the ordering of society, and, one might add, the current battles over the value of life in the unborn and elderly. Third, she would like to see a clarification of the meaning of the priesthood, especially as pertains to the function of the priest and the presence of Christ through the action of the Holy Spirit.

III

But whether Orthodoxy needs modernity is not, probably, the most interesting question to ask. Indeed, it nearly goes without saying that the eastern Church has no choice but to come to terms with, at the very least, the technological, economic, and political revolutions of the past several centuries. The better question is whether or not modernity needs Orthodoxy. Behr-Sigel's answer is clearly a resounding yes. If the modern world is negatively characterized by its frenetic pace, overstimulation, radical individualism and the vulgarization of all things good and beautiful, Orthodoxy could not stand in starker contrast or offer a better counterbalancing antidote.

That is because the first and last thing to be said about Orthodoxy is that it revolves entirely around liturgy. The most important feature of the life in Christ is worship of the Father through the Son with the Holy Spirit. The common life of liturgy colors all else in the life of the Orthodox community; that is why, for instance, the theological works of the Orthodox are nearly always devotional in character and accessible to most catechized lay people. That is also why there are no distinct orders within Orthodox monasticism. It is simply understood that all monastic life takes its cues from the daily worship and everything else is structured around it.

The marriage of discipline and beauty within Orthodox worship is also a timely lesson for the modern world. Here one is confronted with a deep sensuality that for all its richness refuses to pander to the senses. The icons are non-naturalistic and heavily laden with symbolism, refusing fast digestion of their meaning and inviting reflection and prayer. The liturgical melodies are very basic, always a cappella, and the heavy wordiness (to a westerner) of St John Chrysostom's liturgy is repeated week after week, but the repetition forces the words to retain the full extent of their meaning. Complex formulas prevent capitalization by spirituality-hawkers; "Wisdom: let us attend" does not a catchy slogan make. And the worship of Orthodox churches simply does not make sense outside of an ecclesial context. By its nature it evades individualization and requires the common witness of a community.

Even the more private practices, such as meditation and hesychasm, continually draw the "user" back to the life of the community. Behr-Sigel has studied at length the history of hesychasm—the cultivation of inner silence and peace from focusing on the name of Jesus or the Jesus prayer ("Lord Jesus Christ, Son of God, have mercy on me, a sinner")—and has found that its very nature draws one into the ecclesial communion of saints across time. Its long history, stretching all the way back to the desert hermits, anchors the modern Christian, providing a respite from the incessant noise and rootlessness of an industrial world. The prayer, in fact, has been used in much the same way as slave spirituals were in the American South, a repetitive plea for help from above that alleviated the monotony of manual labor for exiled Russians in France. Again, the beauty of an ancient heritage, initially attractive, eludes coercion by the age of advertising because it is inevitably accompanied by the demanding requirements of devotion. At the very least, one is not even permitted to sit during the liturgy: one does not sit in the presence of the King of Kings!

This liturgy is the binding mortar of all the local permutations of Orthodoxy. Despite the embarassing regional disputes and divisions, there is a theological unity in the eastern Church that is simply unheard of in the West, because, finally, all theology comes from the wellspring of the common life of worship. Given the instability of western liturgy across the board, it is no surprise that there is so much factionalism, even within the individual churches. *Lex orandi, lex credendi,* "the rule of prayer is the rule of faith,"after all. In fact, Orthodox theologians have been known to attribute the western penchant for schism ever after to its first serious tampering with the creed of the Council of Nicaea, which, so says the East, resulted in a millennium-long state of trinitarian confusion that could only result in explosive ecclesiological disagreements. The Orthodox have now come to emphasize what the Russians call *sobornost,* commonly translated as "solidarity" though it was originally coined by Sts Cyril and Methodius as the Slavonic word for "catholicity," which could well become the basis for Orthodox ecumenical intiatives.

Once again, it is in the controversial matter of women in the Church and in the world that Behr-Sigel sees great potential for Orthodoxy's universal contribution. Here is a Church that remains almost completely untouched by the women's movement—feminism has never been a great attraction for Orthodox women, or at least the feminism they have seen in the West—so the next few steps Orthodoxy takes toward confronting this externally posed challenge are crucial. Not only that, but this is the one big chance for the Church to get the "woman thing" right the first time around.

That implies, of course, a criticism of how the West has handled the women's movement. Behr-Sigel makes no bones about it. She attributes many of the unfortunate and unfaithful extremes of corrupted western women's movements to a fearful refusal by the Church to assess the genuinely true and good impulse behind them. In the company of other Orthodox theologians, such as Evdokimov and Bukharev, she discerns instead a very serious and Spirit-driven challenge to the Christian world. She explains: "The contemporary women's movement (rather than the 'feminist' movement) is, in spite of its weaknesses, a sign of that secret and irresistible force of the Spirit that is lifting humanity toward the Kingdom of the life-giving Trinity. This movement is certainly an ambiguous and sometimes irritating sign, written in clumsy letters and spoken of in consciously provocative terms, a sign of 'a Christian idea gone haywire' in our Far West that finds itself submerged by a nihilistic tidal wave... The women's movement participates both in the violence and in the noble hope that is the divine image in man. Despite its excesses, the women's movement asks serious questions of the churches."

The serious questions, for the Orthodox, naturally begin with the aforementioned church practices and have extended to the character of the priesthood. For the modern world at large, though, the feminine witness—and for Behr-Sigel, its expression in Orthodox theo-anthropology—both poses a challenge and offers hope. Behr-Sigel suspects that, where the modern world has sown the seeds of its potential downfall, it has also planted the possibility of its own regeneration. "Here and now," she speculates, "could there not be an authentic dialogue between men and women that would bring about the renewal of the aborted dialogue in the West between humanism and faith? In place of a Cartesian humanism of the male, "master and possessor of the earth," we must substitute a new humanism pervaded with respect for the other, with tenderness and compassion for mankind and the whole of God's creation." She asks, in a characteristic rhetorical flourish, "Would not a genuinely feminine presence in all domains of culture, including the concrete life of our ecclesial communities, contribute to such a humanism?" Imagine: a philosophical revolution provoked by the priorities of wives, mothers, monastics, and children. And yet—Behr-Sigel is always careful to specify—this is not intended to be a softer, kinder instance of feminist disdain for masculinity. Following the pattern of the Church Fathers once again, she insists that the human creature is essentially a "conjugal" being: the partnership of male and female is the basic unit for understanding all human relationships and endeavors in the world. For Behr-Sigel, then, the corrective role of the feminine ethos, harnessed and channeled by the Church, is to check an aggressive masculinity spun out of control by the unlimited power and opportunities of the modern world. She writes: "Let us hope that women can help men against themselves, against their deformed masculinity which women carry in themselves too, to stop humanity at the edge of the abyss and to stop the destruction of history."

But to do this—to fulfill its vocation—the women's movement must engage in unflinching self-examination of its failings thus far, and furthermore, reflect seriously on what it aspires to be. For Behr-Sigel, there is no question of rejecting old stereotypes only to replace them with new ones, or permitting the more common error in her tradition that would use so-called feminine charisms as an excuse for keeping women out of real participation and responsibility in the Church. Indeed, the life of the Church plays a crucial role in understanding afresh woman's role in salvation history, especially when the world at large, through its scientific and industrial breakthroughs, has rendered the roles once assigned to women by nature and tradition in large part obsolete. Left to its own secular devices, the women's movement has no choice but to become feminist, then misogynist, and finally atheist and nihilist—no surprise when women feel compelled to break with both God and men in order to retain any sense of honor for their own female selves. On this turn of events in much of western feminism, Behr-Sigel remarks, "Women's demands have their origins in New Testament preaching, in the revolutionary proclamation of the equal dignity in Christ of men and women... However, the women's movement, being cut off from its spiritual roots and being secularized and made profane, has become 'feminist' and in the process has caused a deep and widely spread identity crisis." Whatever the factual truth of feminist criticisms of tradition and society, they can only take away: they cannot create. Here again she sees the opportunity for Orthodox theology to play a restorative role. Behr-Sigel remarks, "Rethought and brought up to date, the Orthodox theo-anthropology could help the women's movement to keep from getting bogged down in an aggressive and wounding militancy."

For Behr-Sigel, all these lines of thinking about woman and man, women and men, finally culminate in Mary. In the person of Mary, the question of women's favor before God is indisputably settled: she is full of grace, visited by the angel and the Holy Spirit, and within her finite female body resides the infinite Redeemer of the world. But—and this is crucial—the mistake is to limit Mary only to her significance for women or her embodiment of supposed feminine charisms. Rather, Behr-Sigel asserts, she is the first in the Church; as a mother, as *the* mother, she teaches by the example of her whole life, from the annunciation to her sorrow at the cross to her prayers with the apostles, what it means to give birth to Christ, not only physically but spiritually as well. Women are called to freely and responsibly imitate Mary in their openness to the divine and their acceptance of Christ's life in them—and so are men. Mary is "a sign of the kingdom already come, of the creation already saved," and this sign is not reserved for Mary's sisters alone but her brothers as well. Together in the Church, men and women are the bride, the beloved, who are wooed by the lover who is God. And so in contrast to the almost exclusively negative use of the word "feminization," Mary is the living model of the femininity to which all people are positively called.

Drawing on the model of the Theotokos, Behr-Sigel assures that "there is no question, certainly, of making men effeminate any more than of turning women into viragos, but it may just be that we want to feminize human beings, in the most noble meaning of the world, to preserve and awaken in them a feminine attitude of effacement and of acceptance when confronted by mystery, the mystery of God and the mystery of the neighbor, the mystery of the Other that I cannot come to know except by opening myself to Him." If such a project were truly carried out, impelled by the Spirit, "a new art of living could bloom, even if it were only on a few islands, like the first Christian communities or medieval monasteries. These communities would be places where being would have priority over having, where inner fulfillment would be more important than competing for power, and where science and technology would serve life, not death." In essence, then, the two persons who make the one human creature are meant not to battle but to teach one another: virile masculinity toward sin and the devil, receptive femininity toward God, and holy love toward one another. If Behr-Sigel's vision carries the day, the Church may cautiously hope for as much.